Africa

Adult Coloring Book

Alisa Calder

First edition: 2017

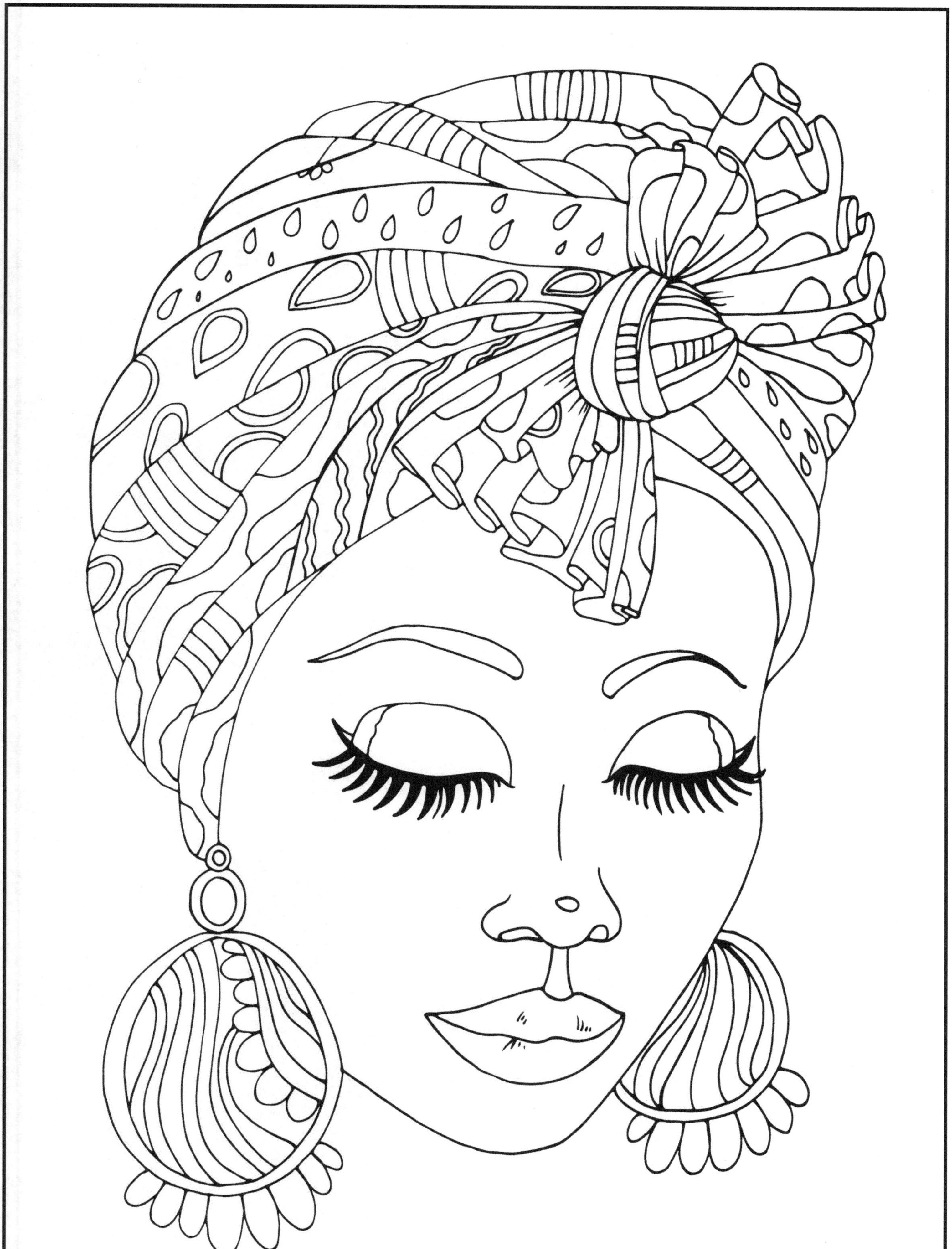

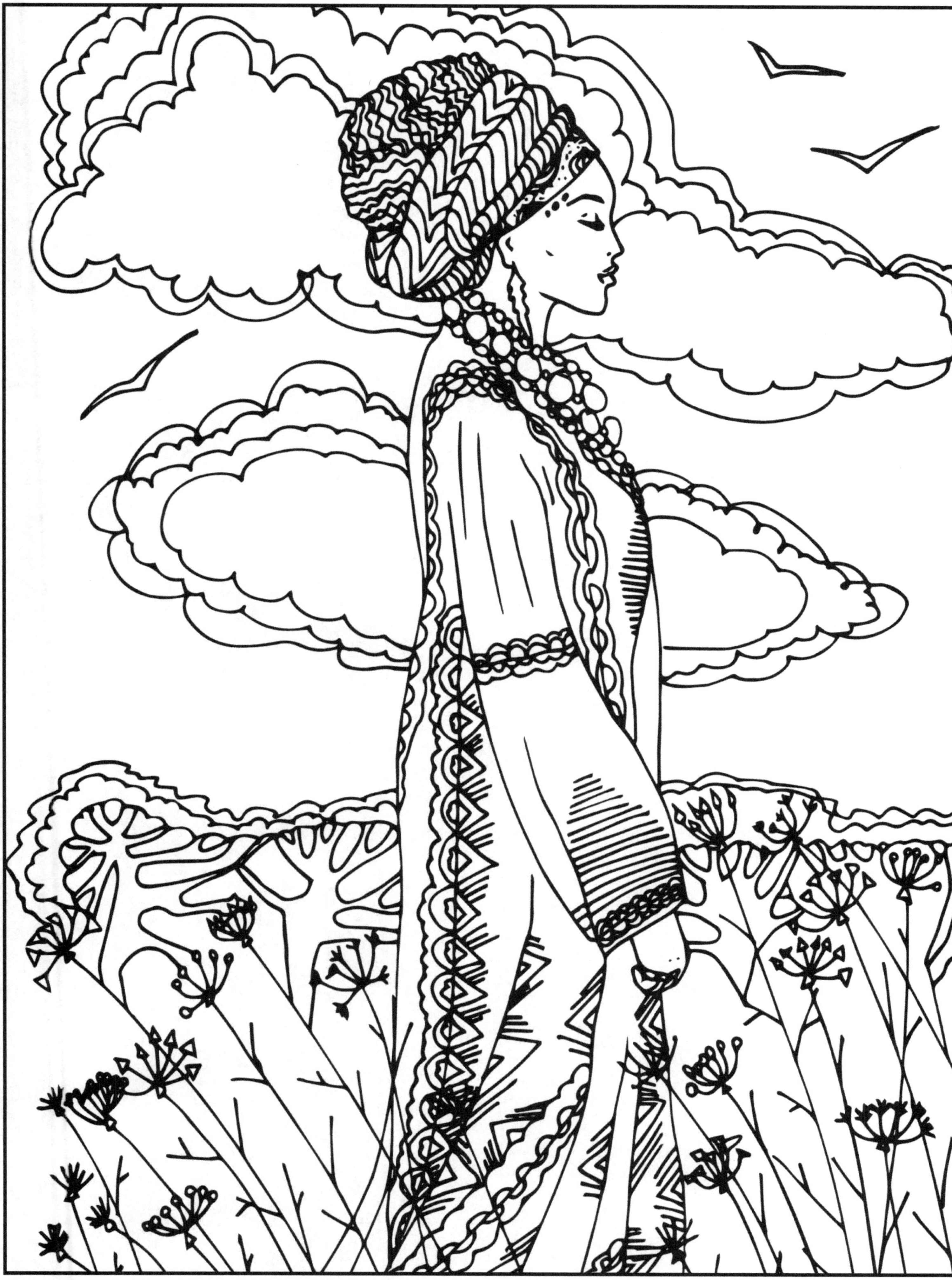

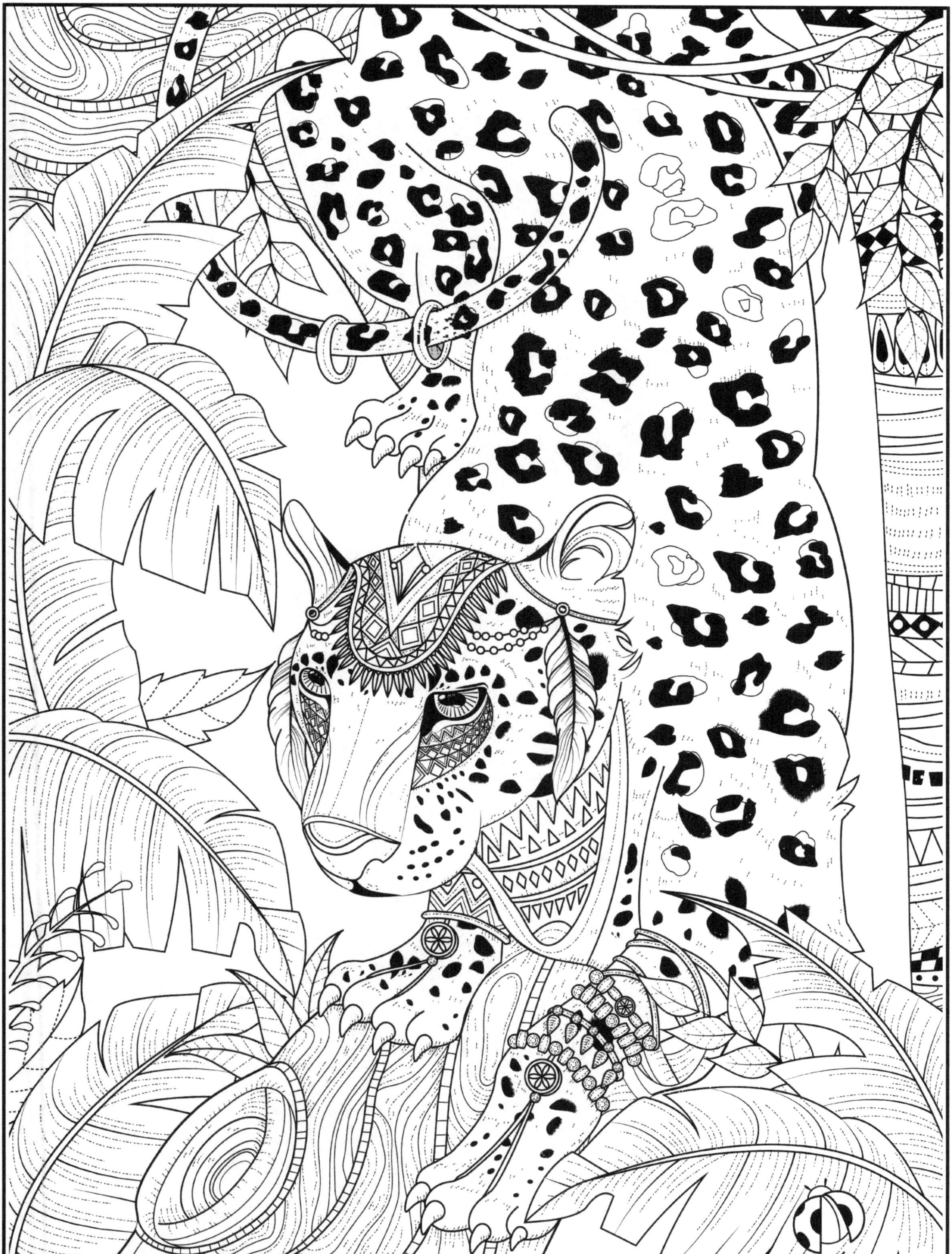

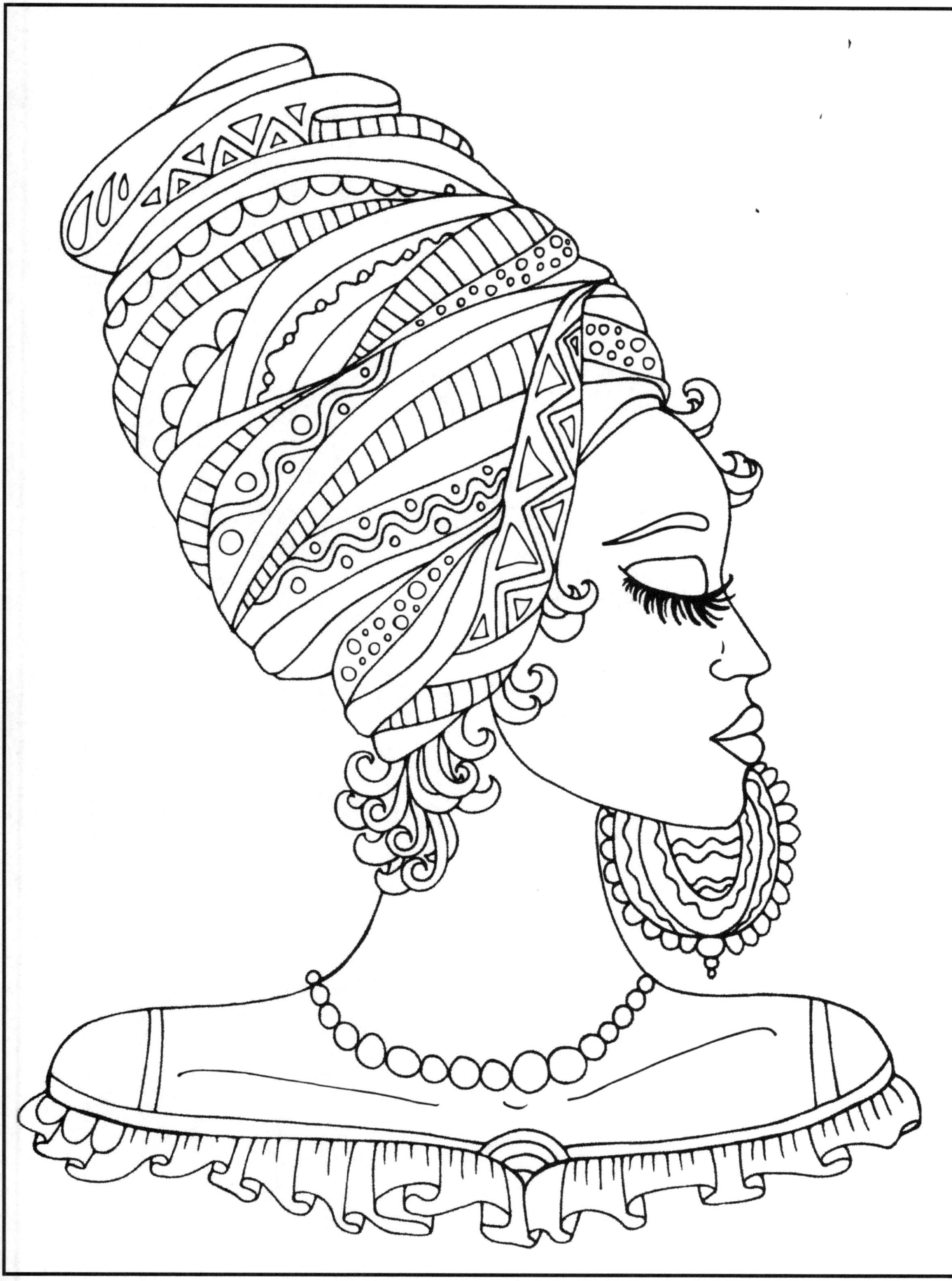

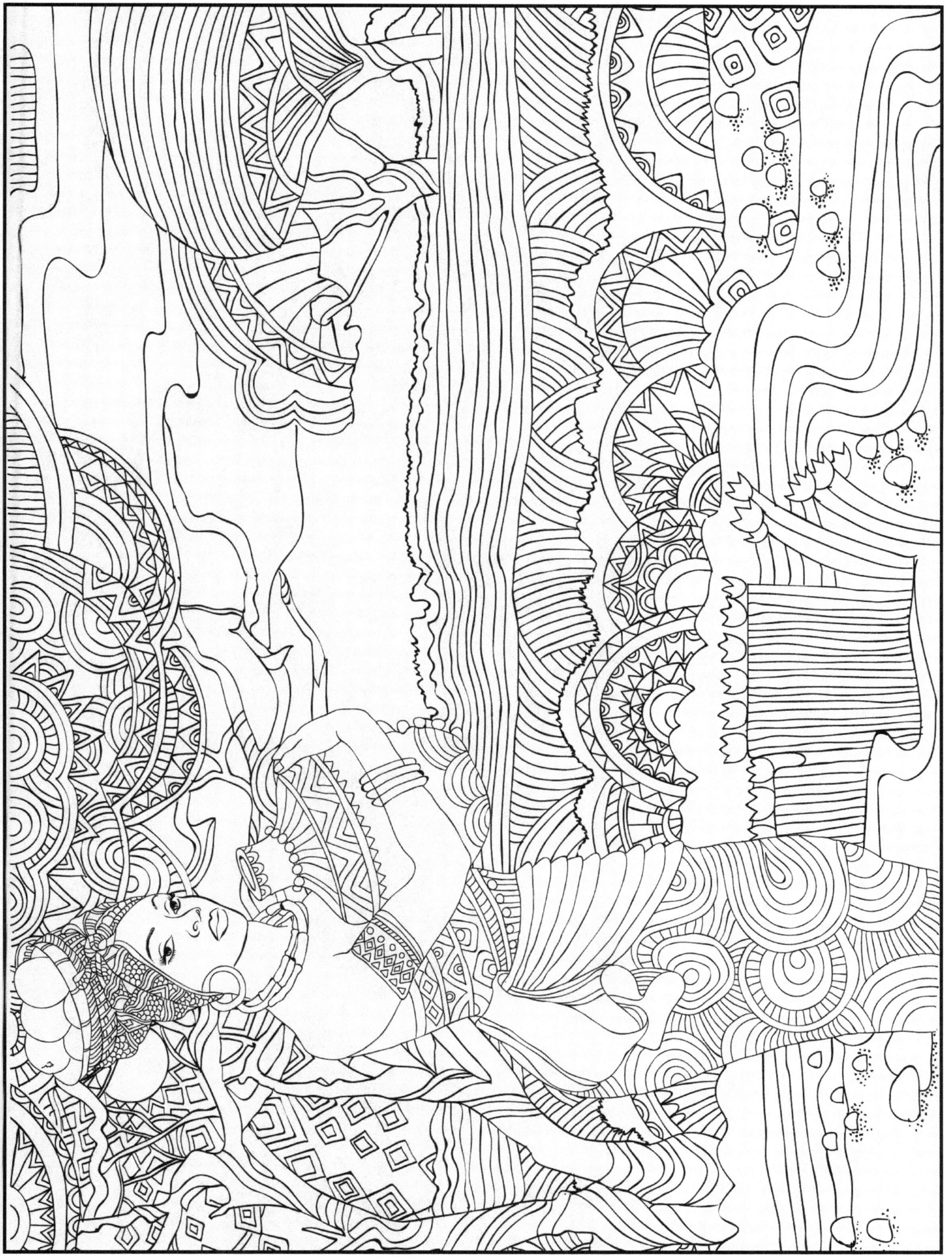

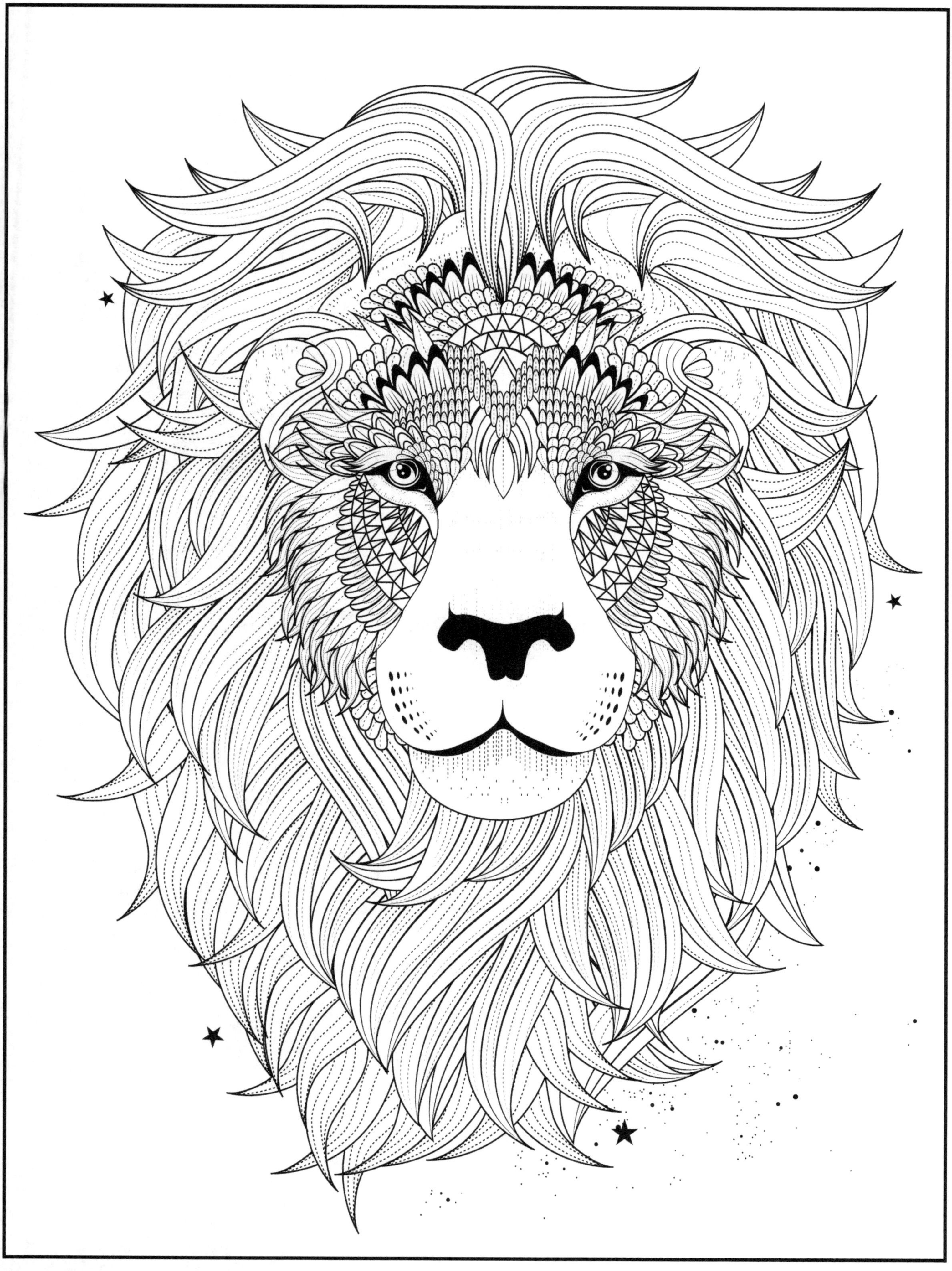

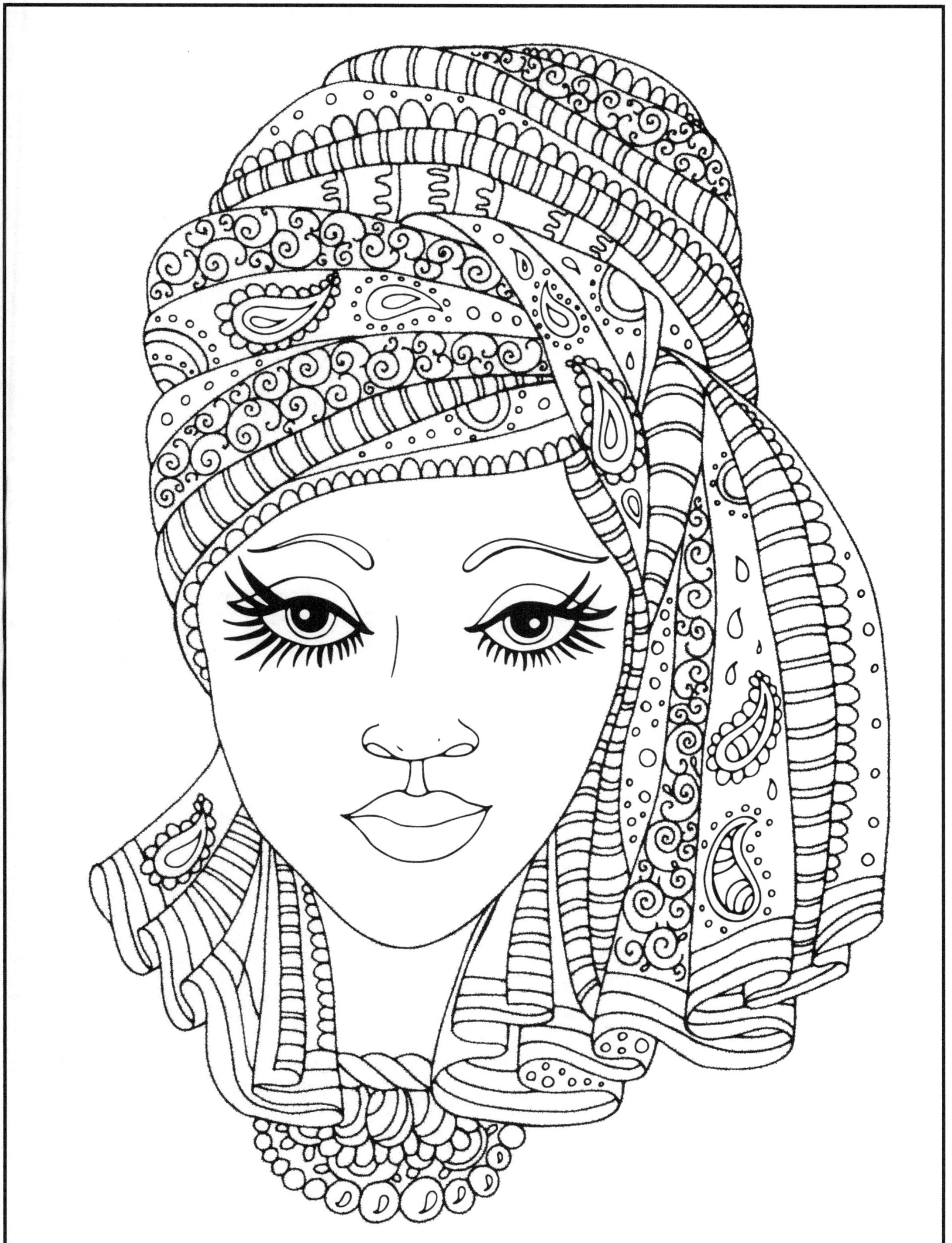

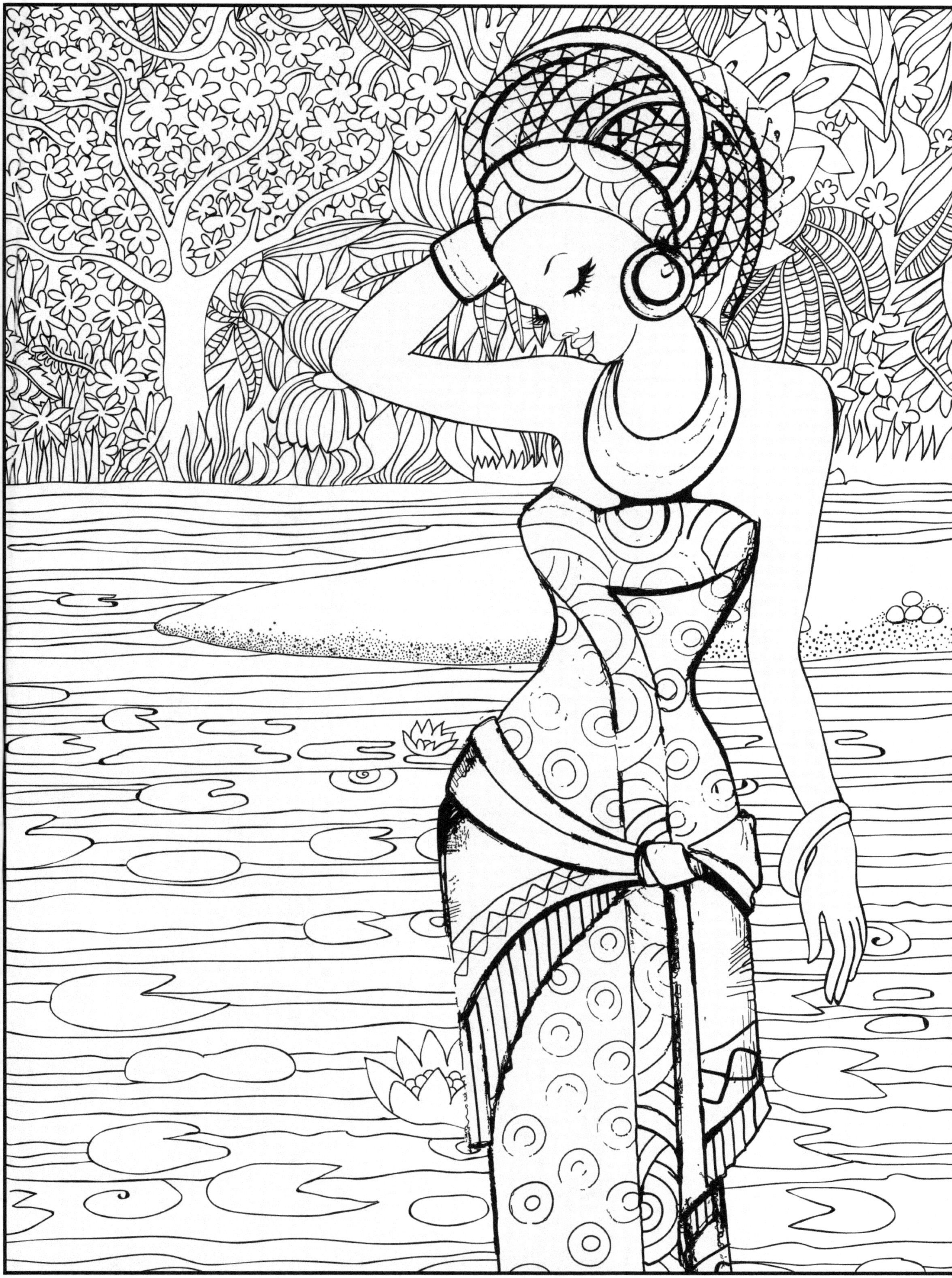

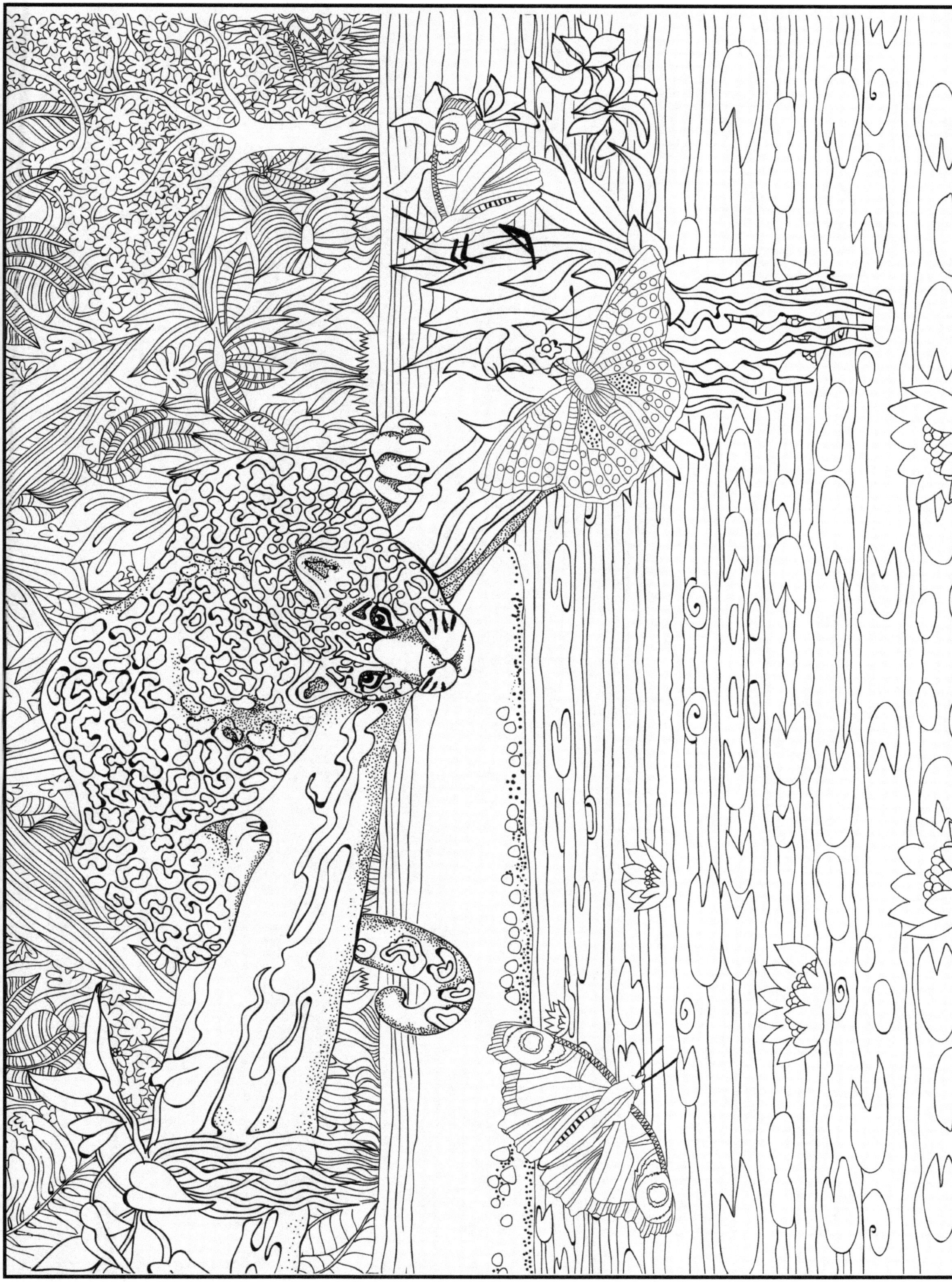

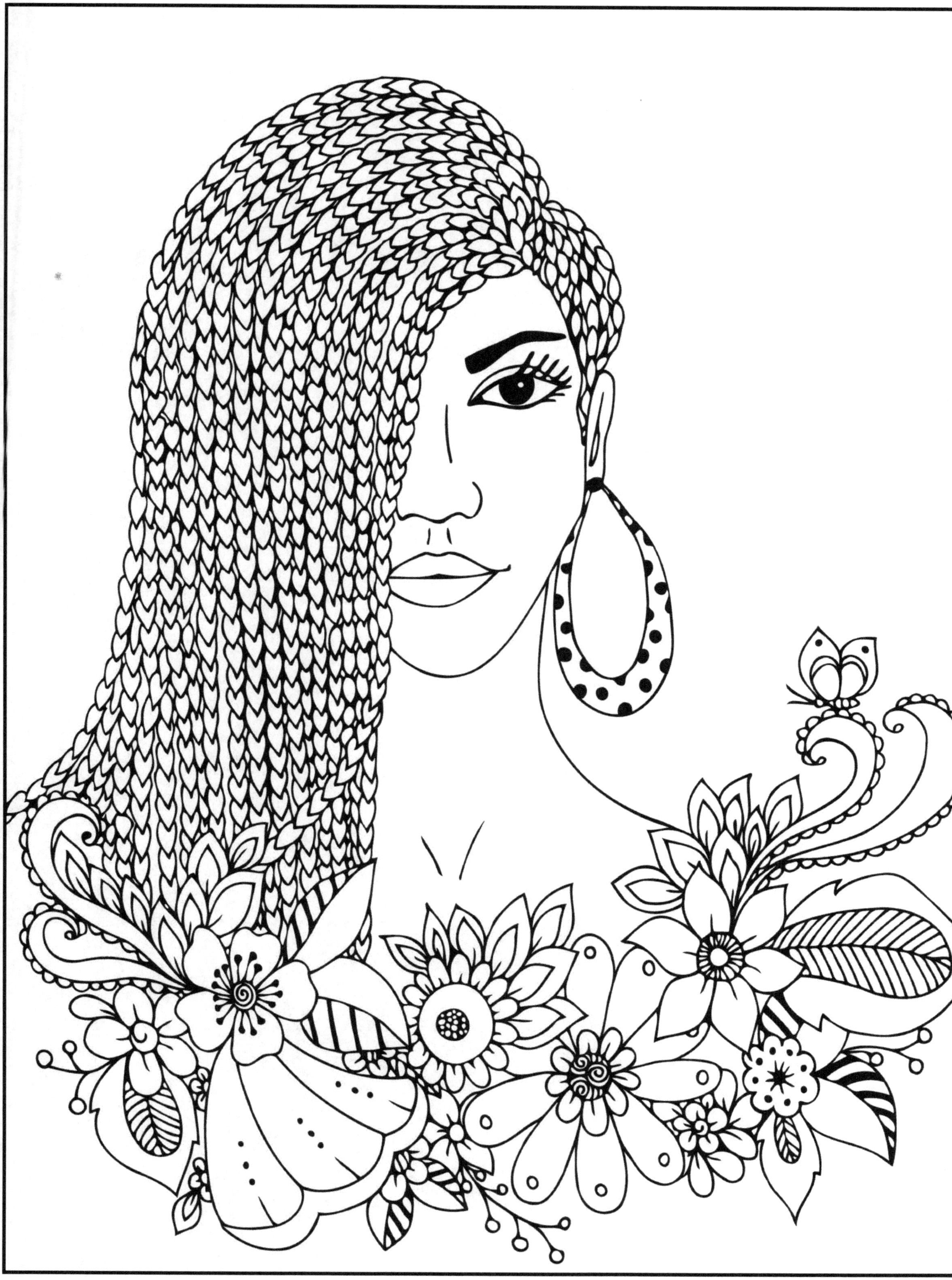

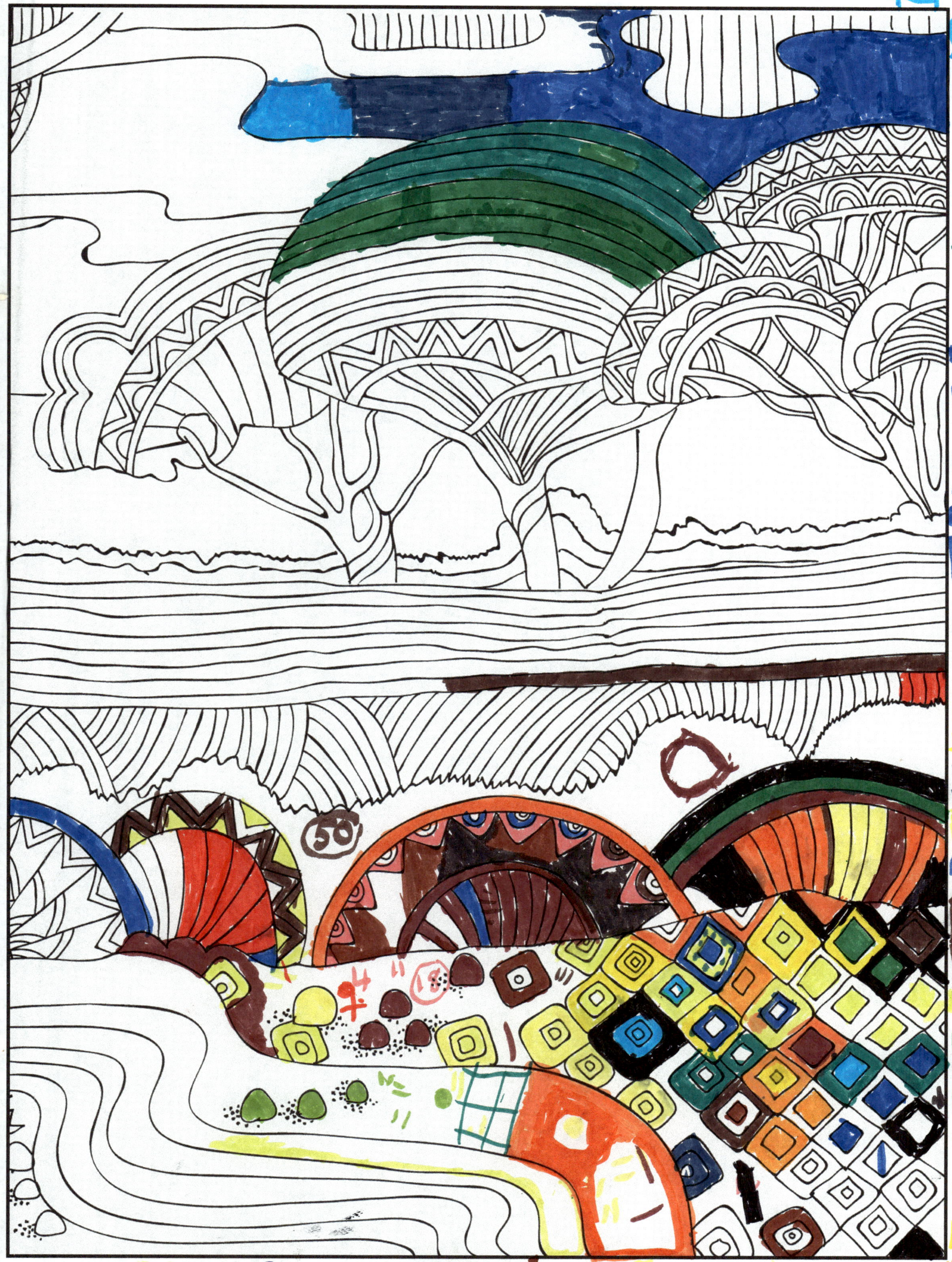

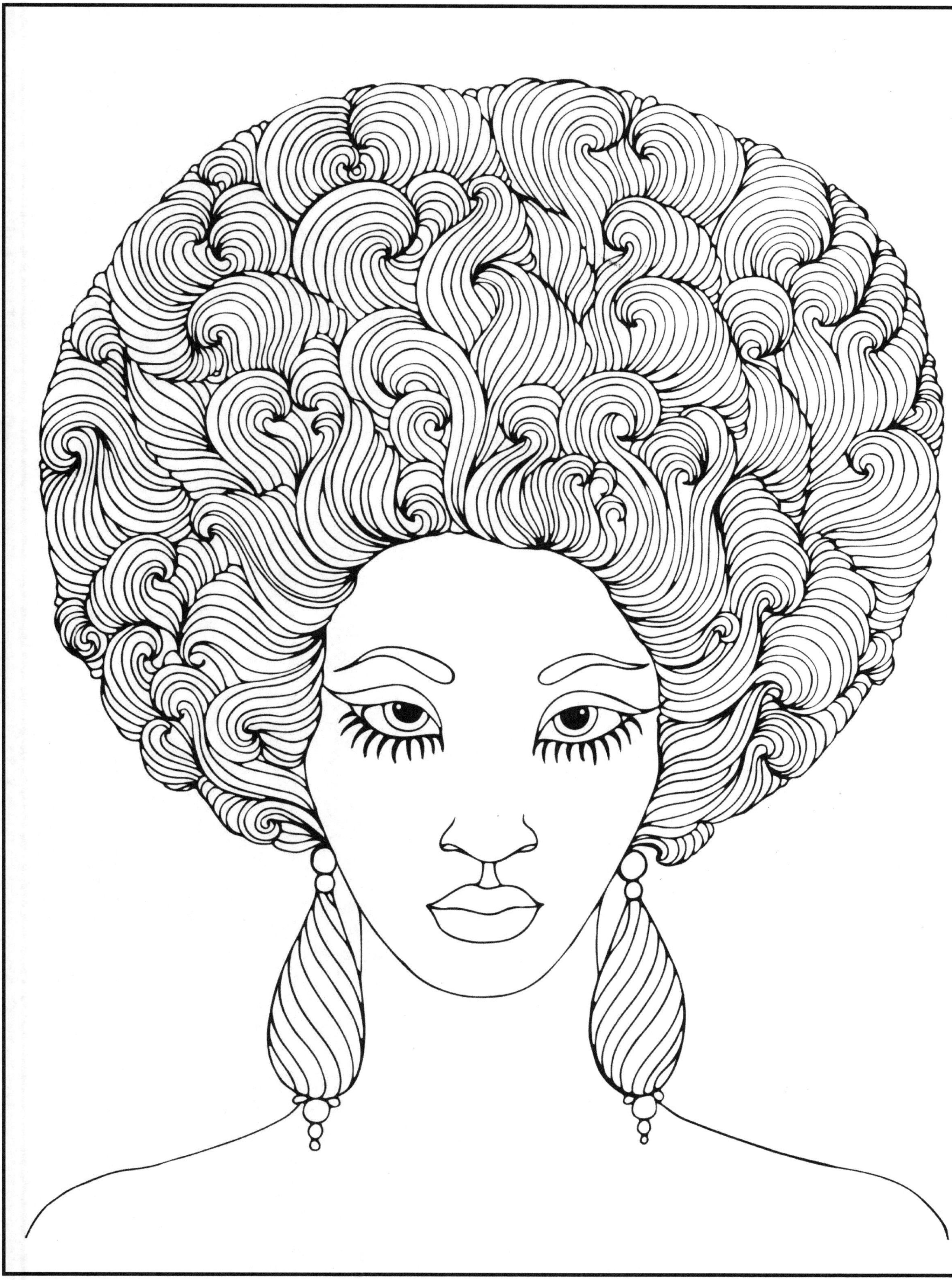

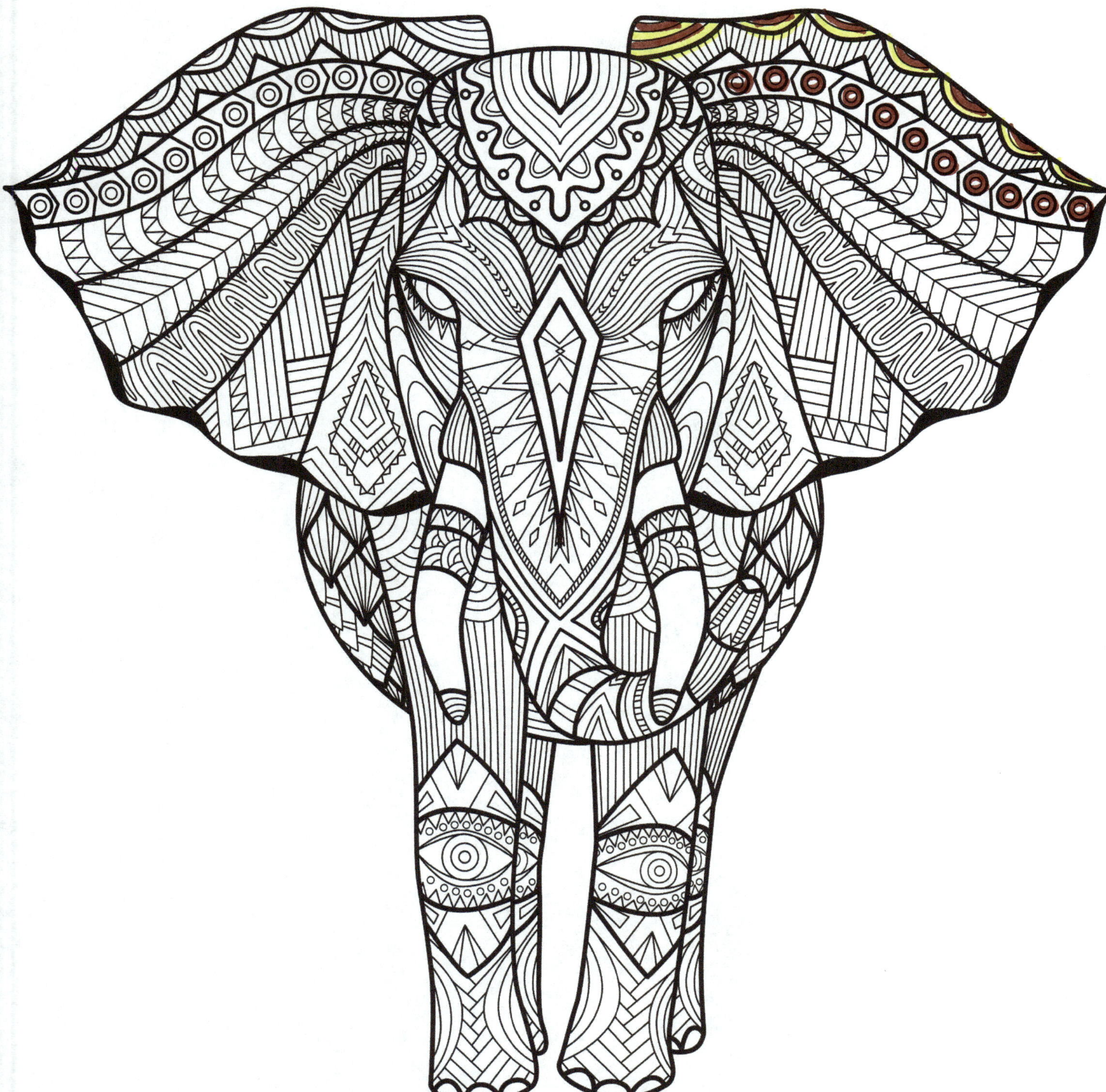

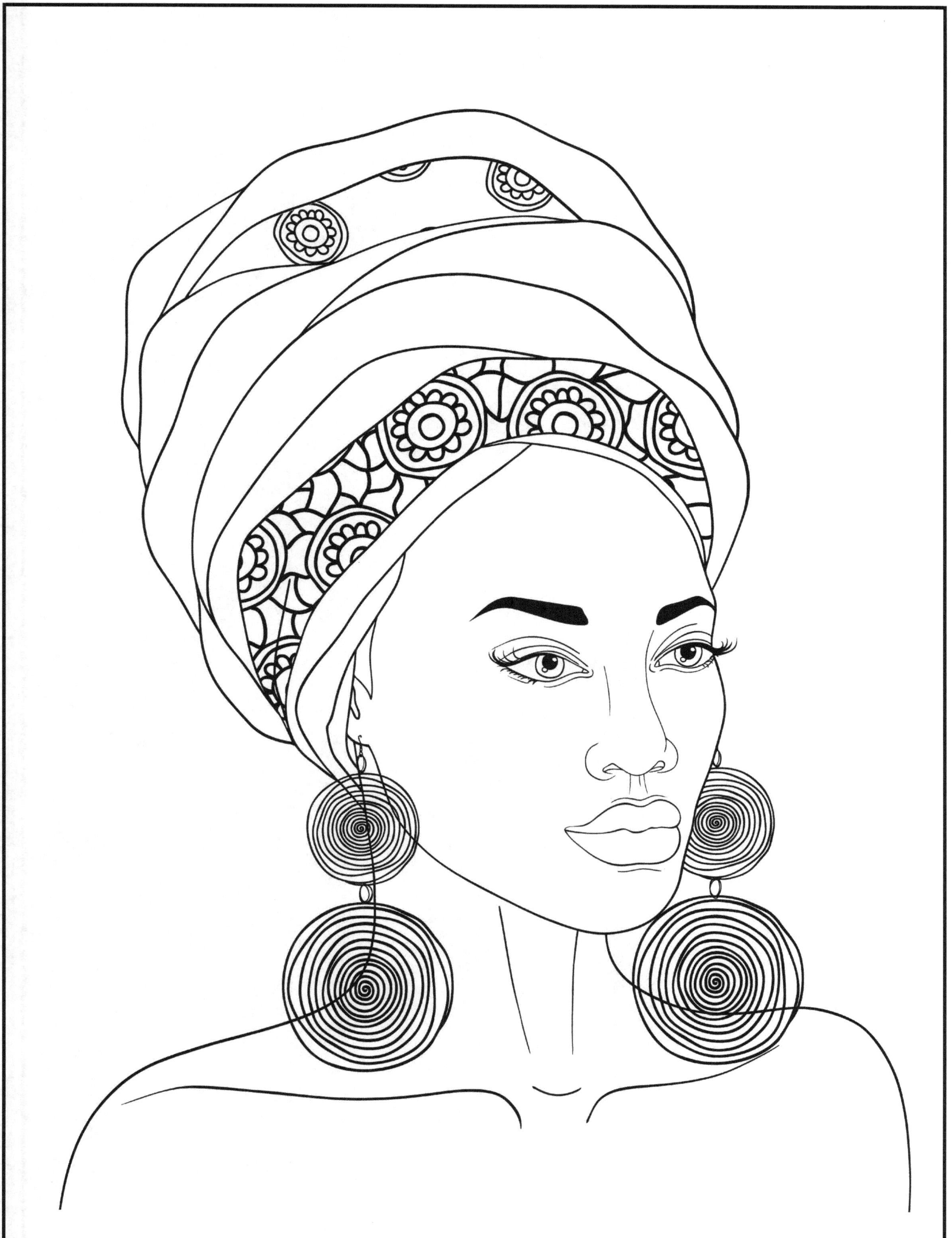

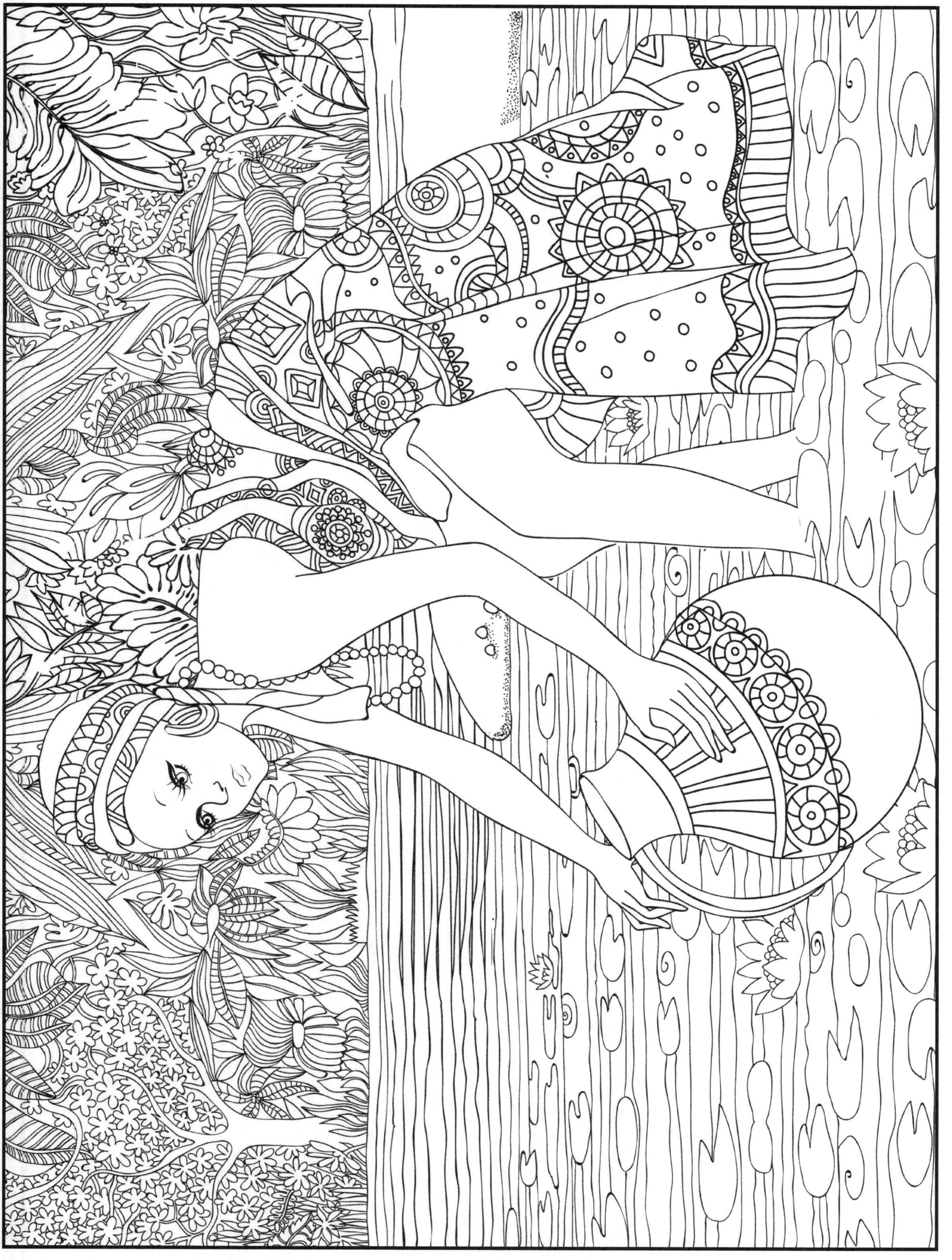

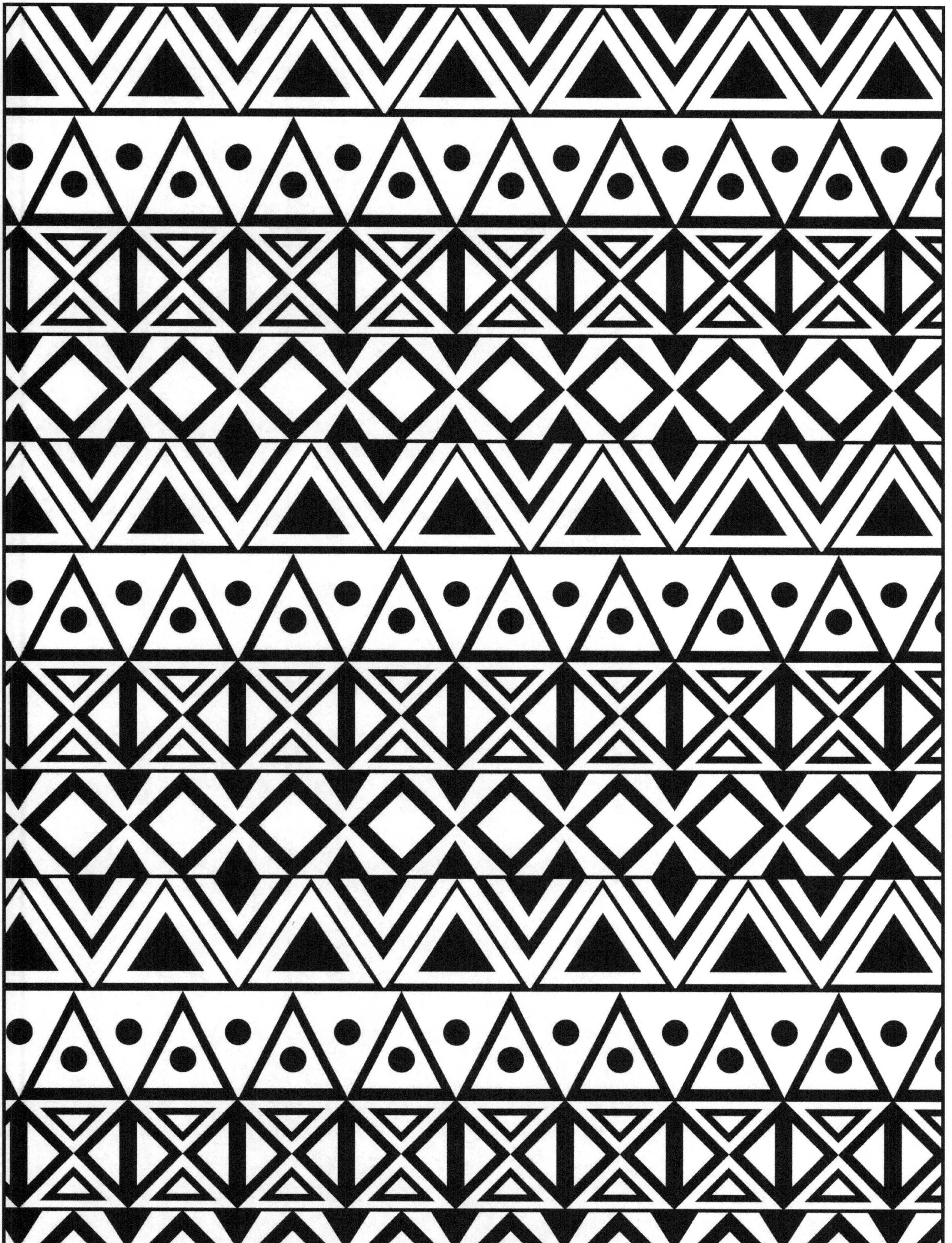

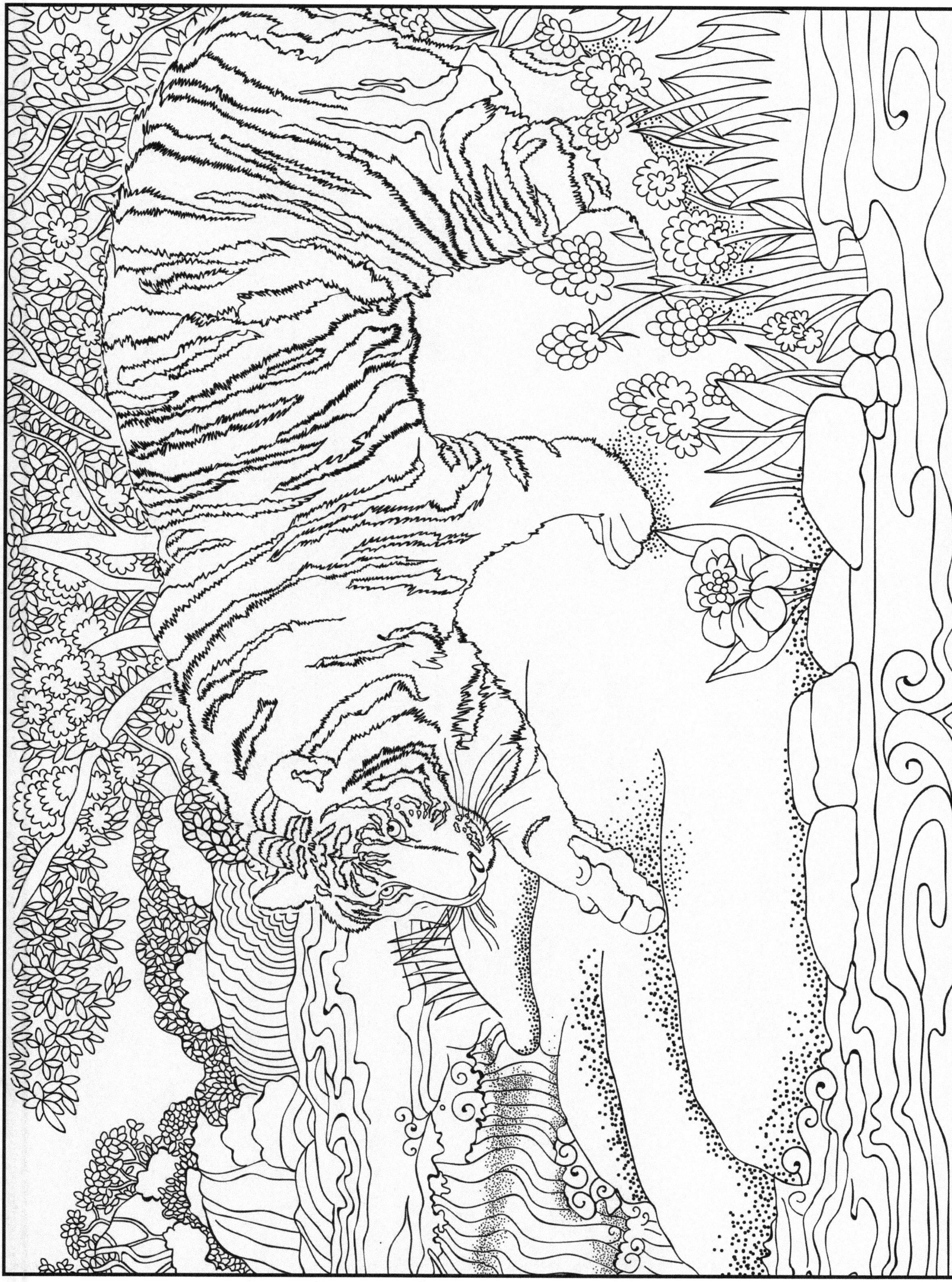

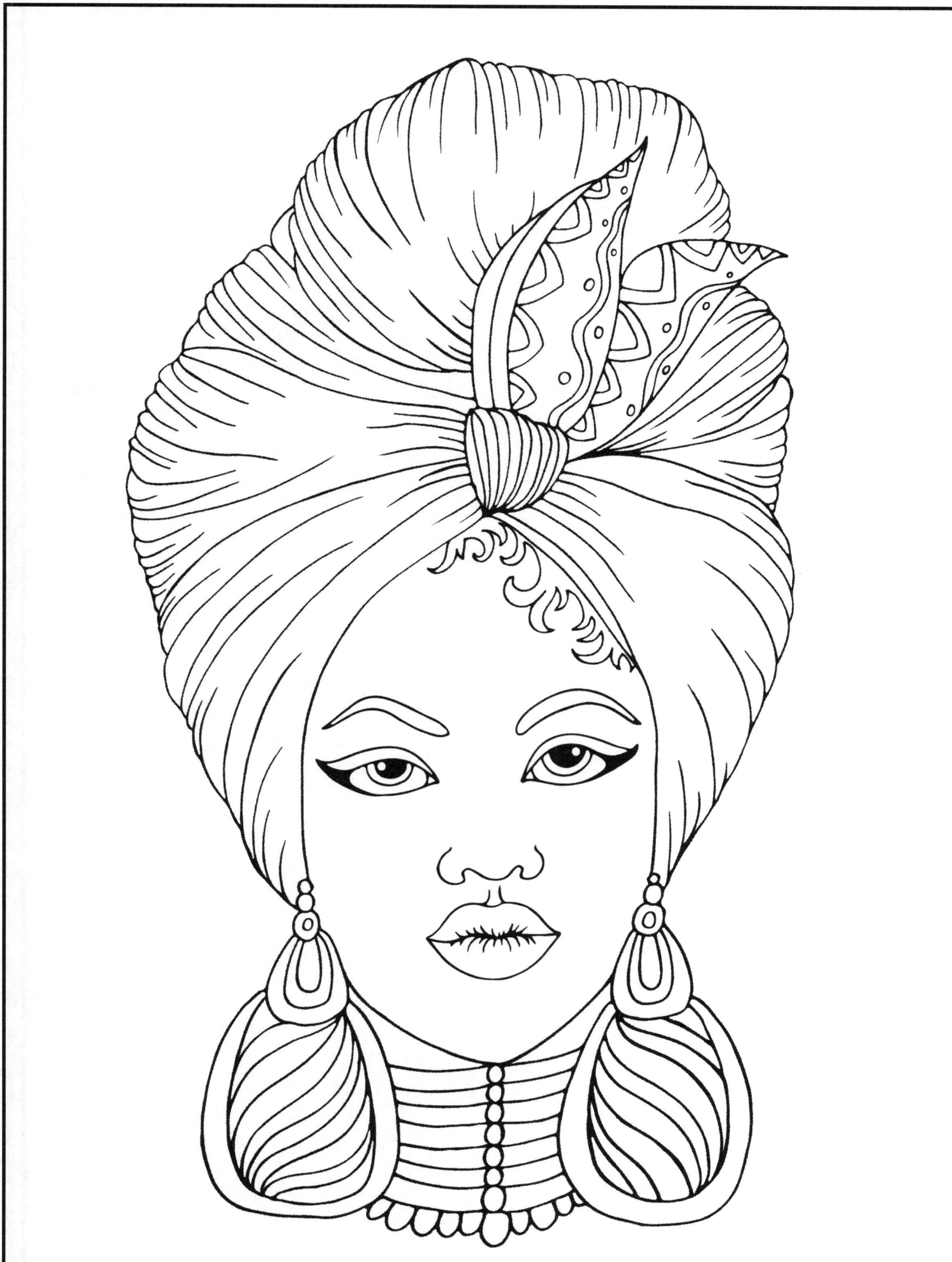

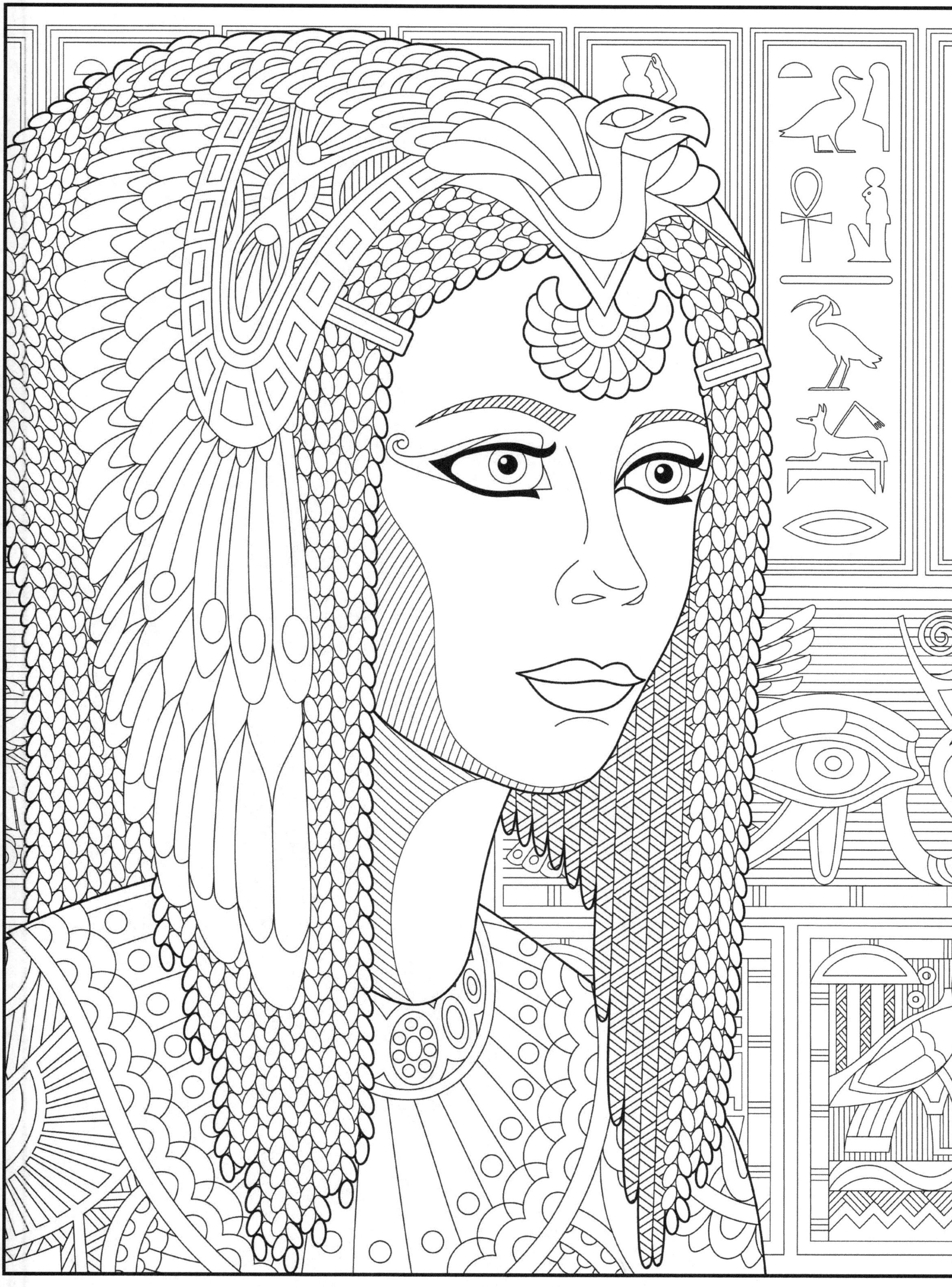

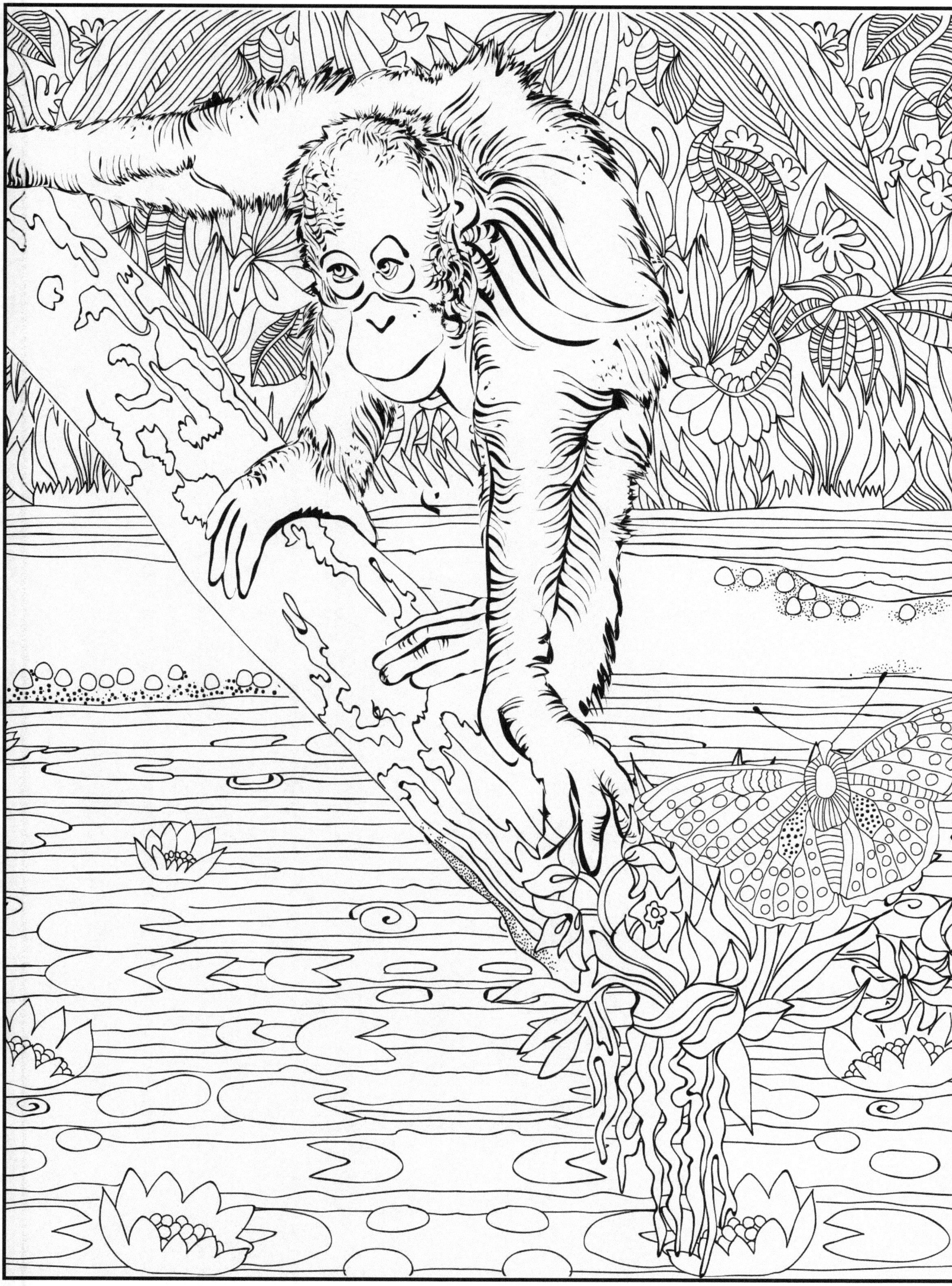

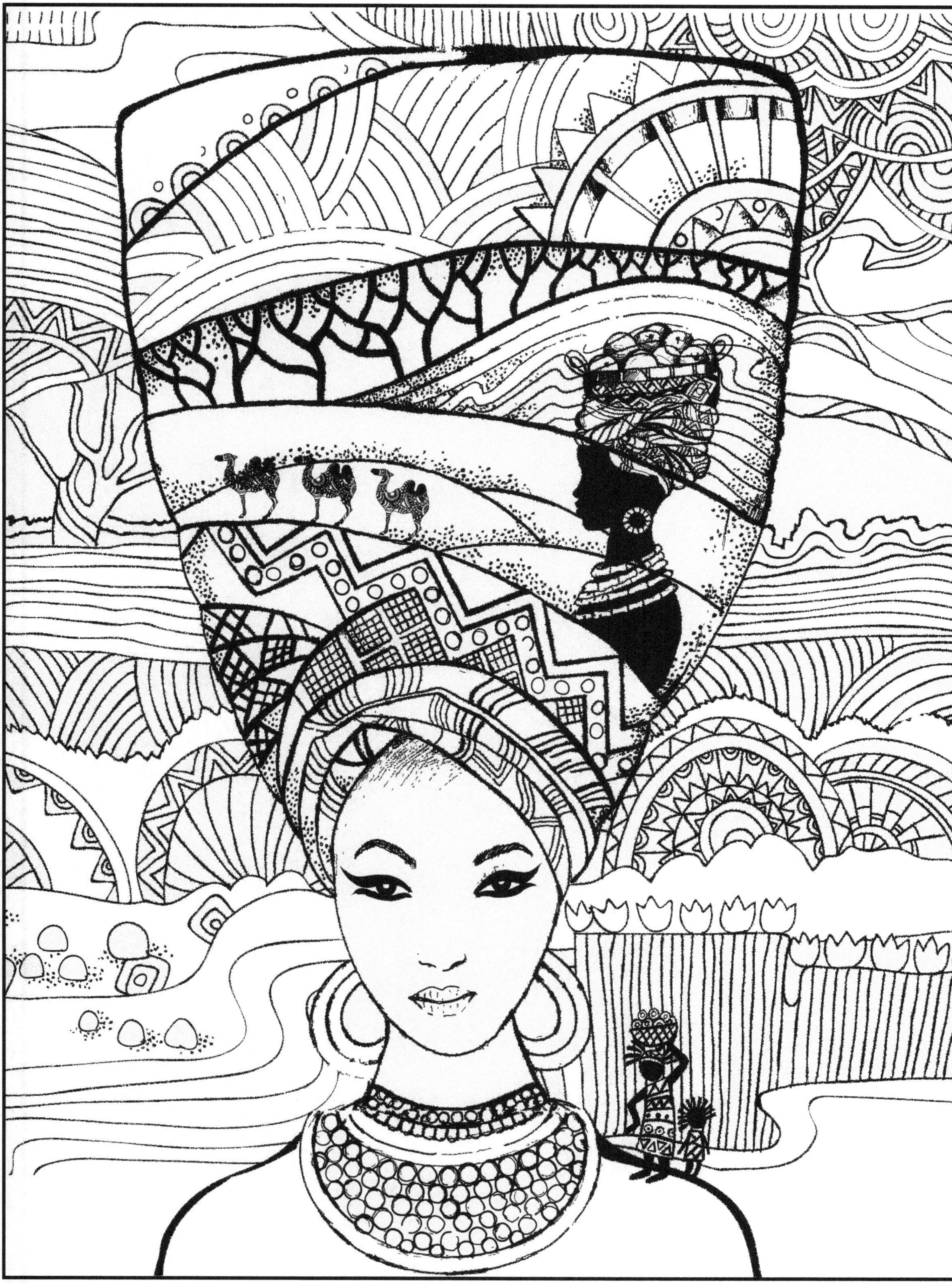

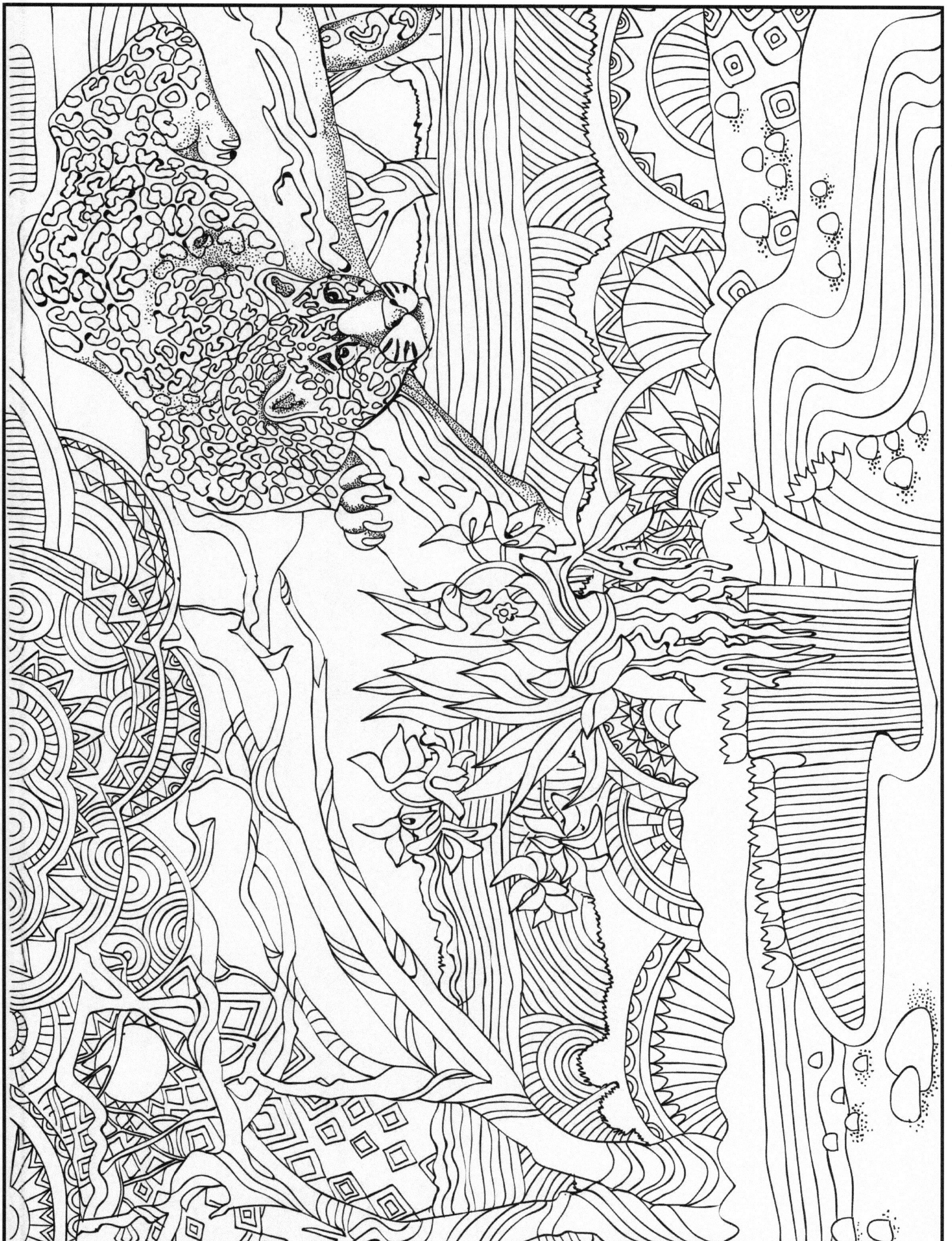

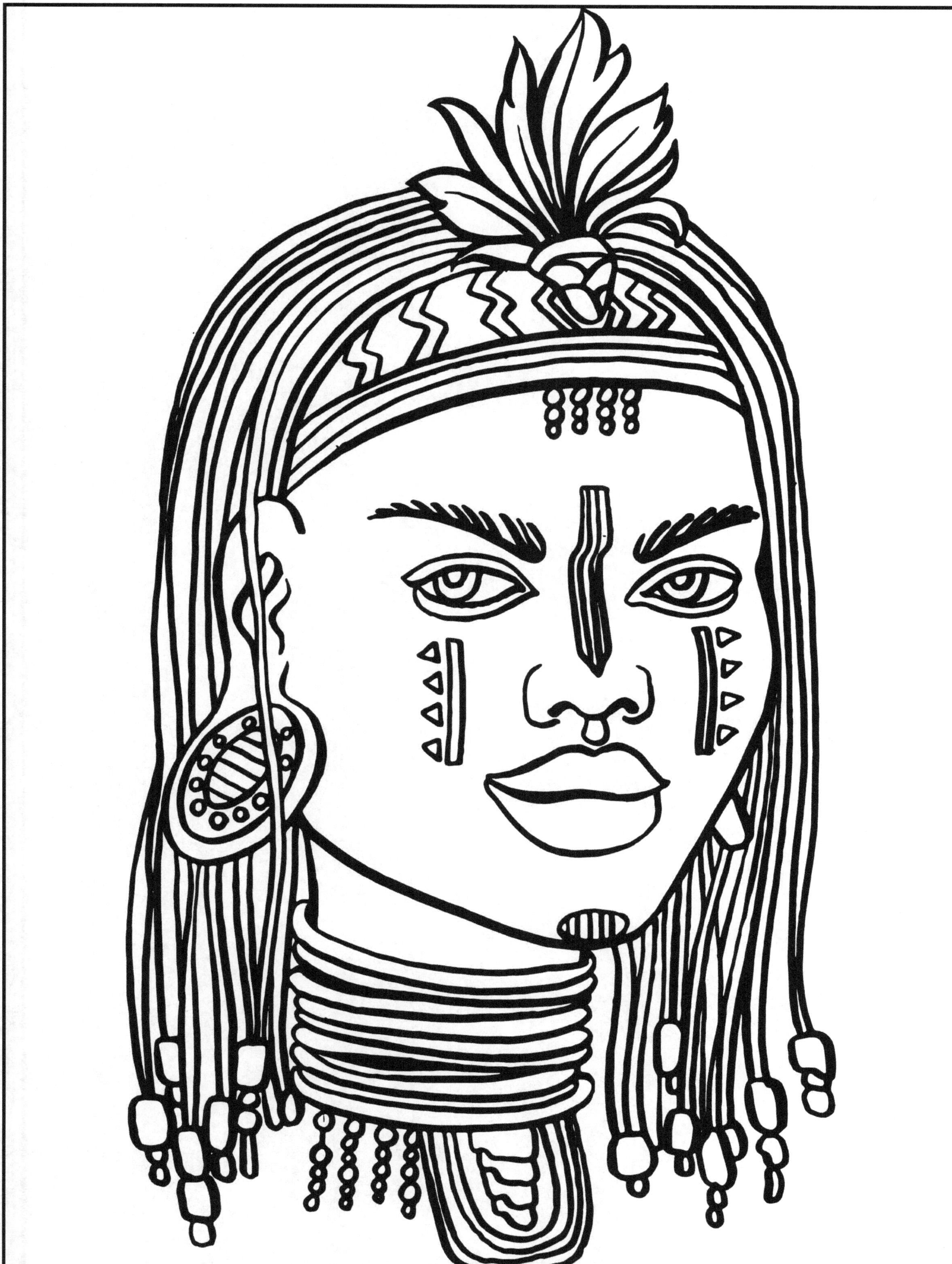

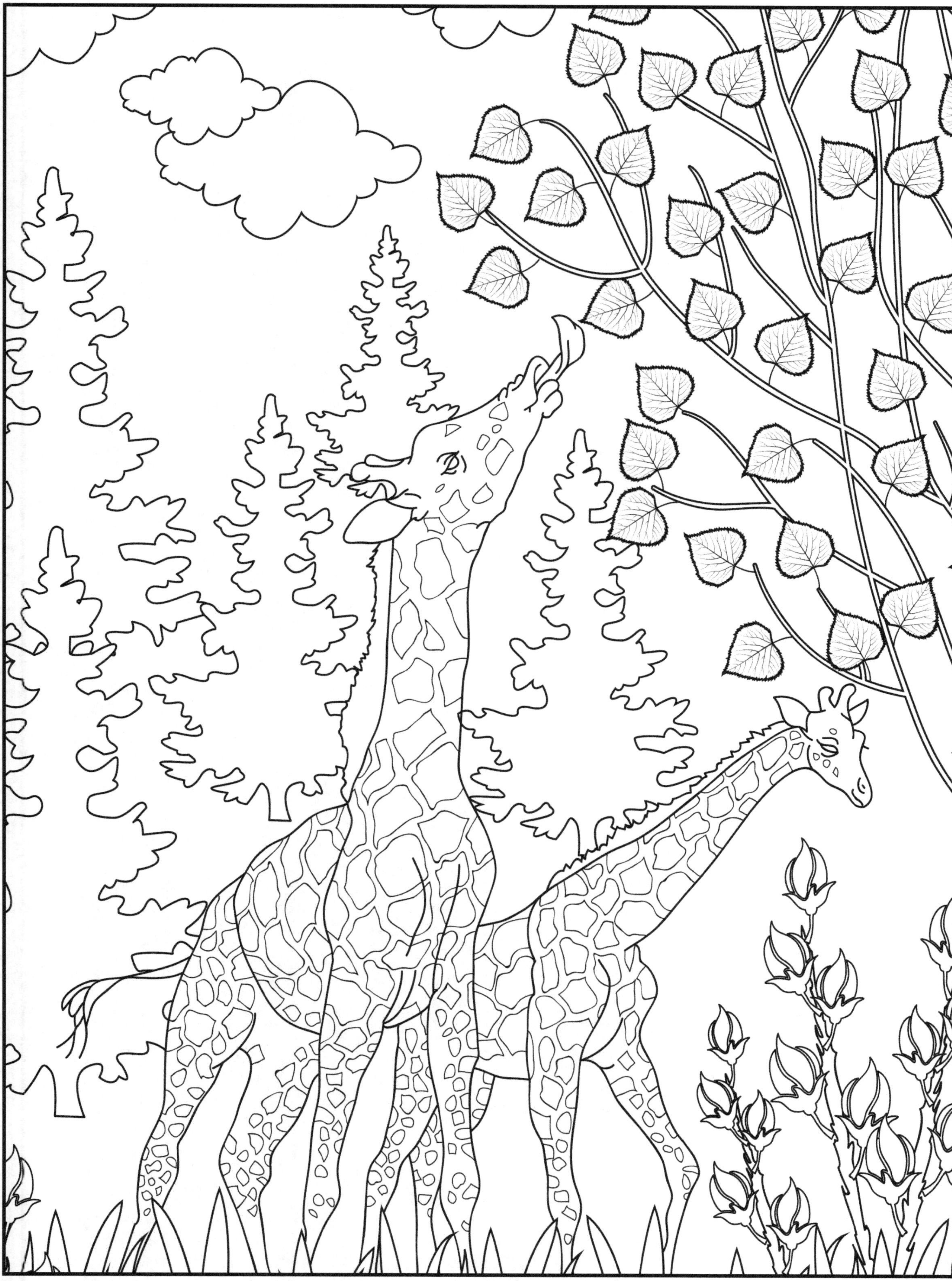

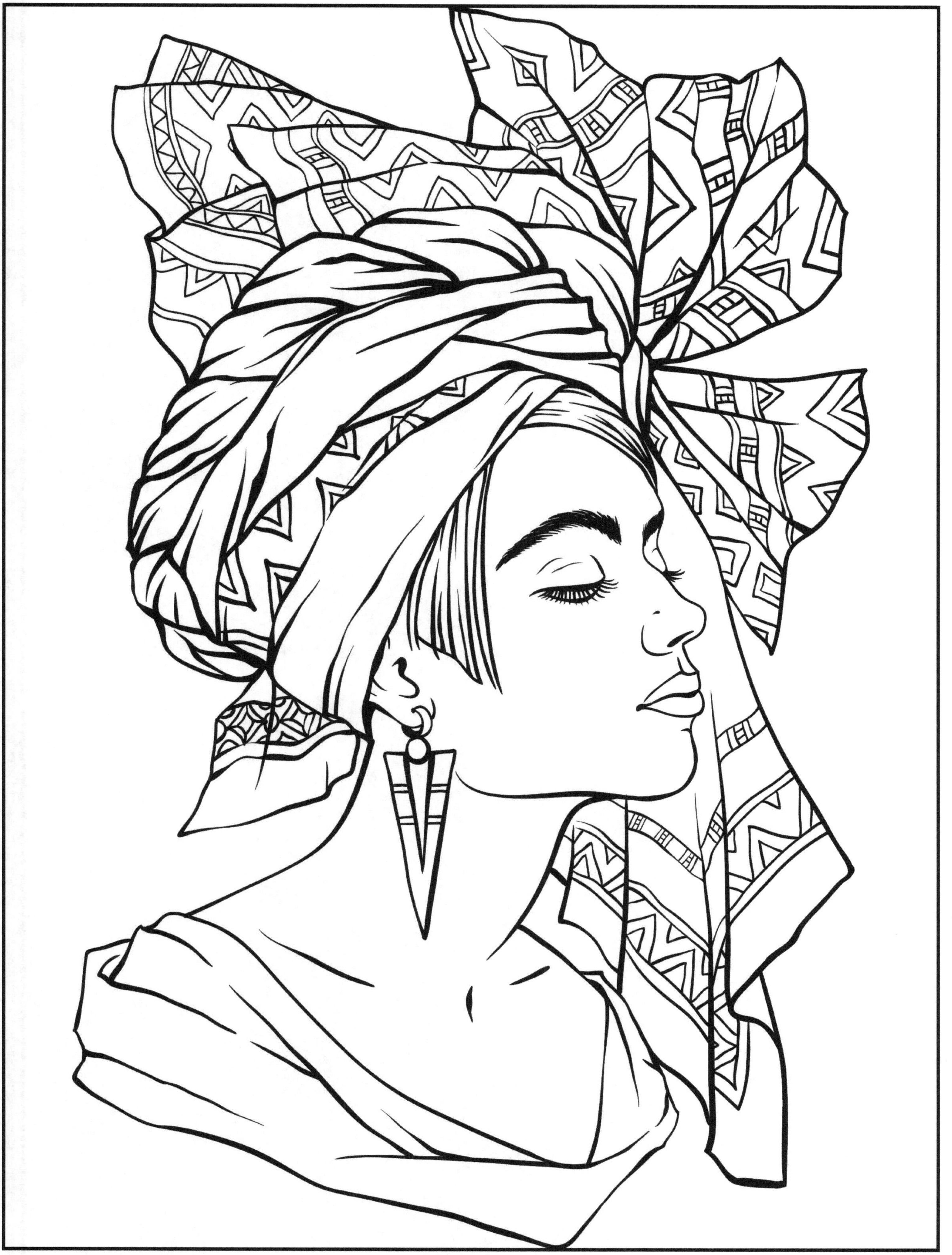

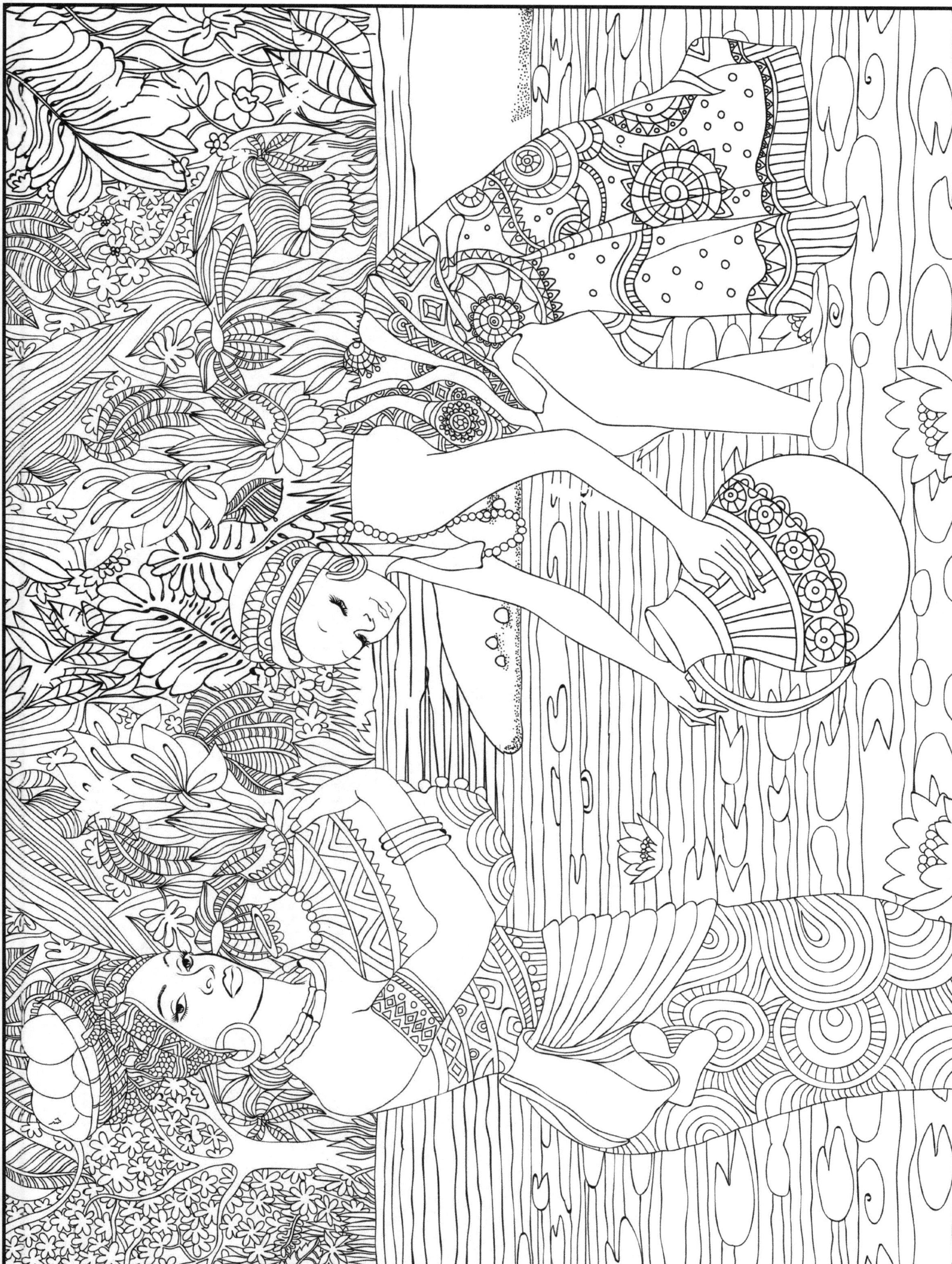

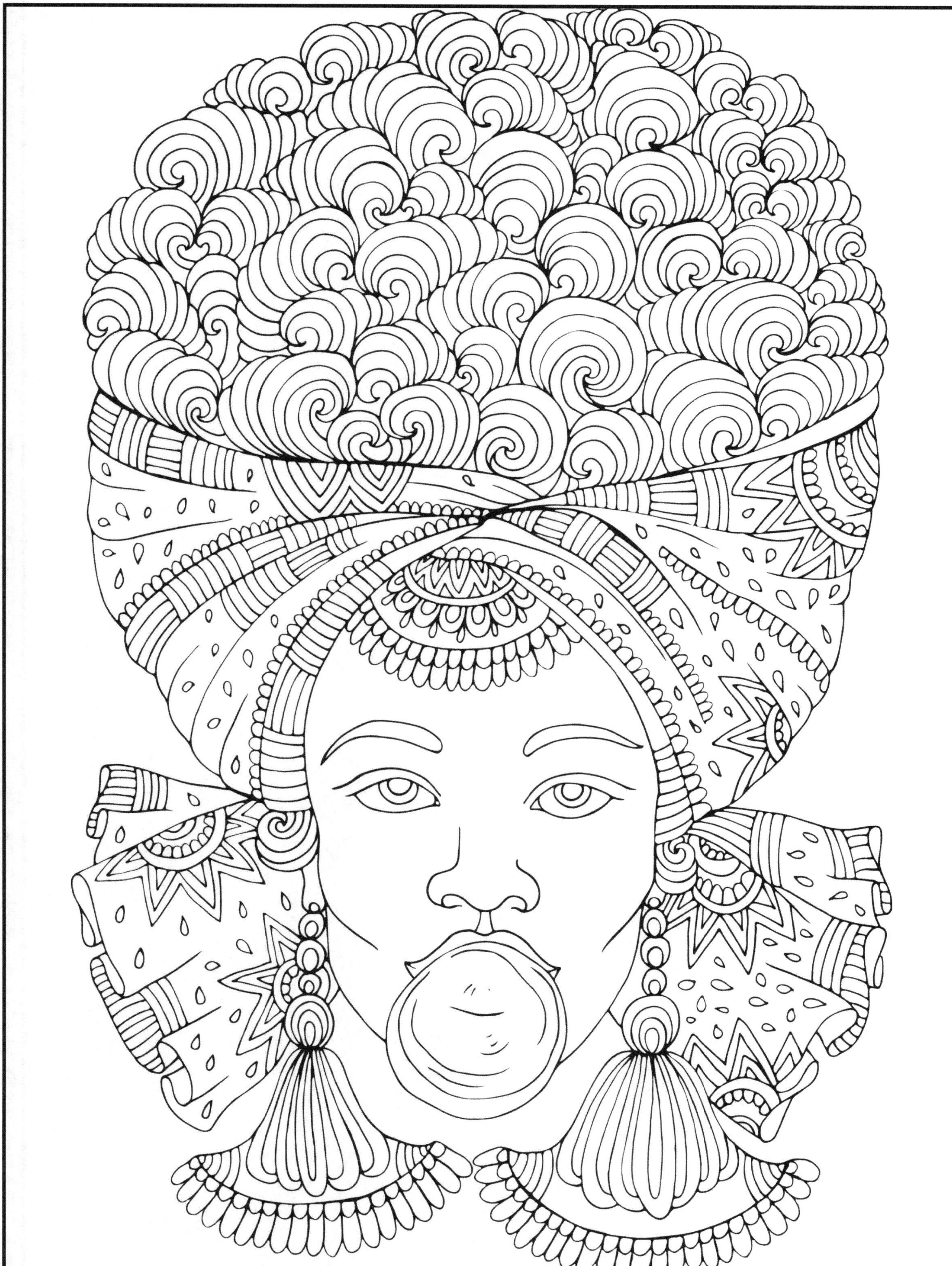

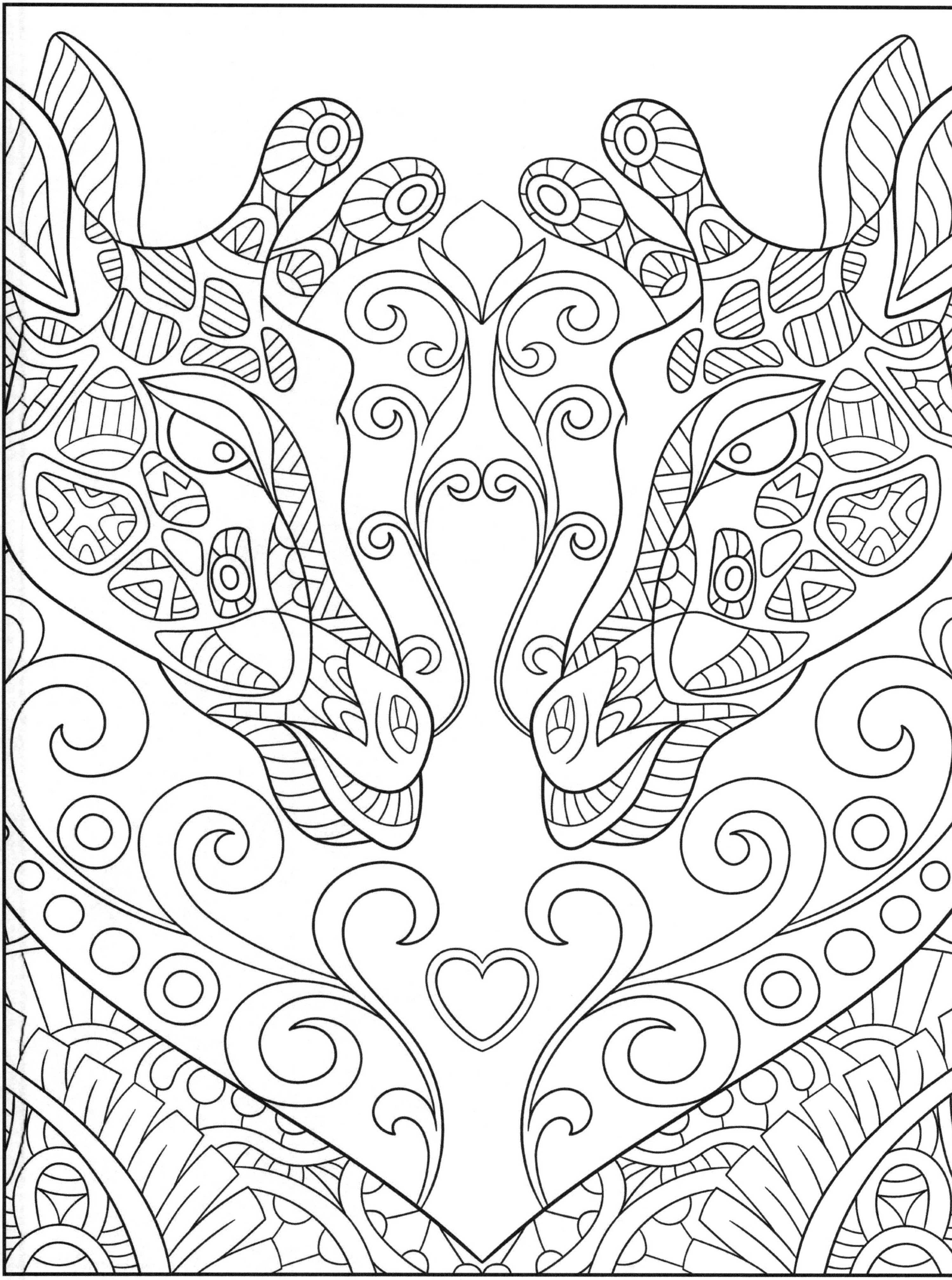

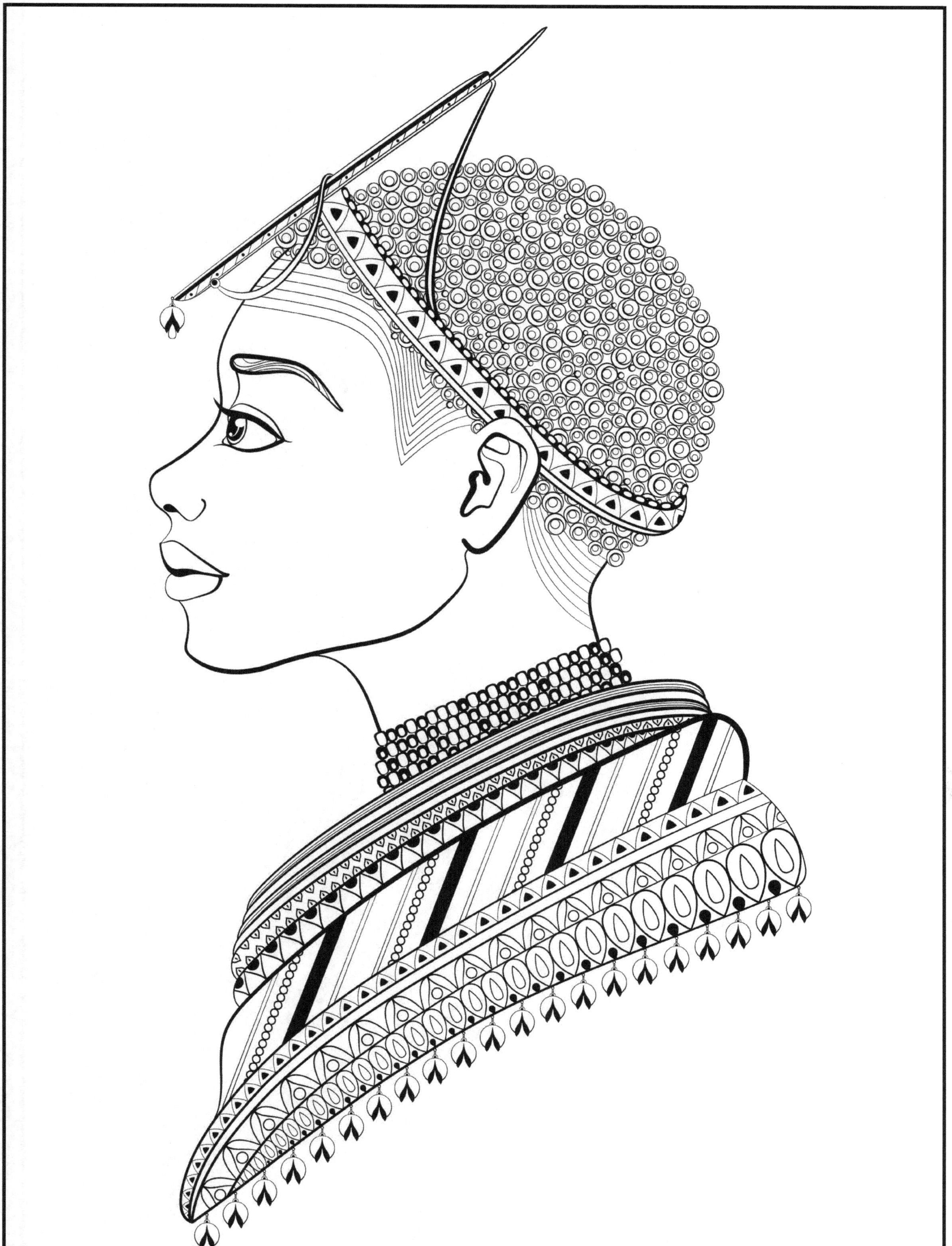

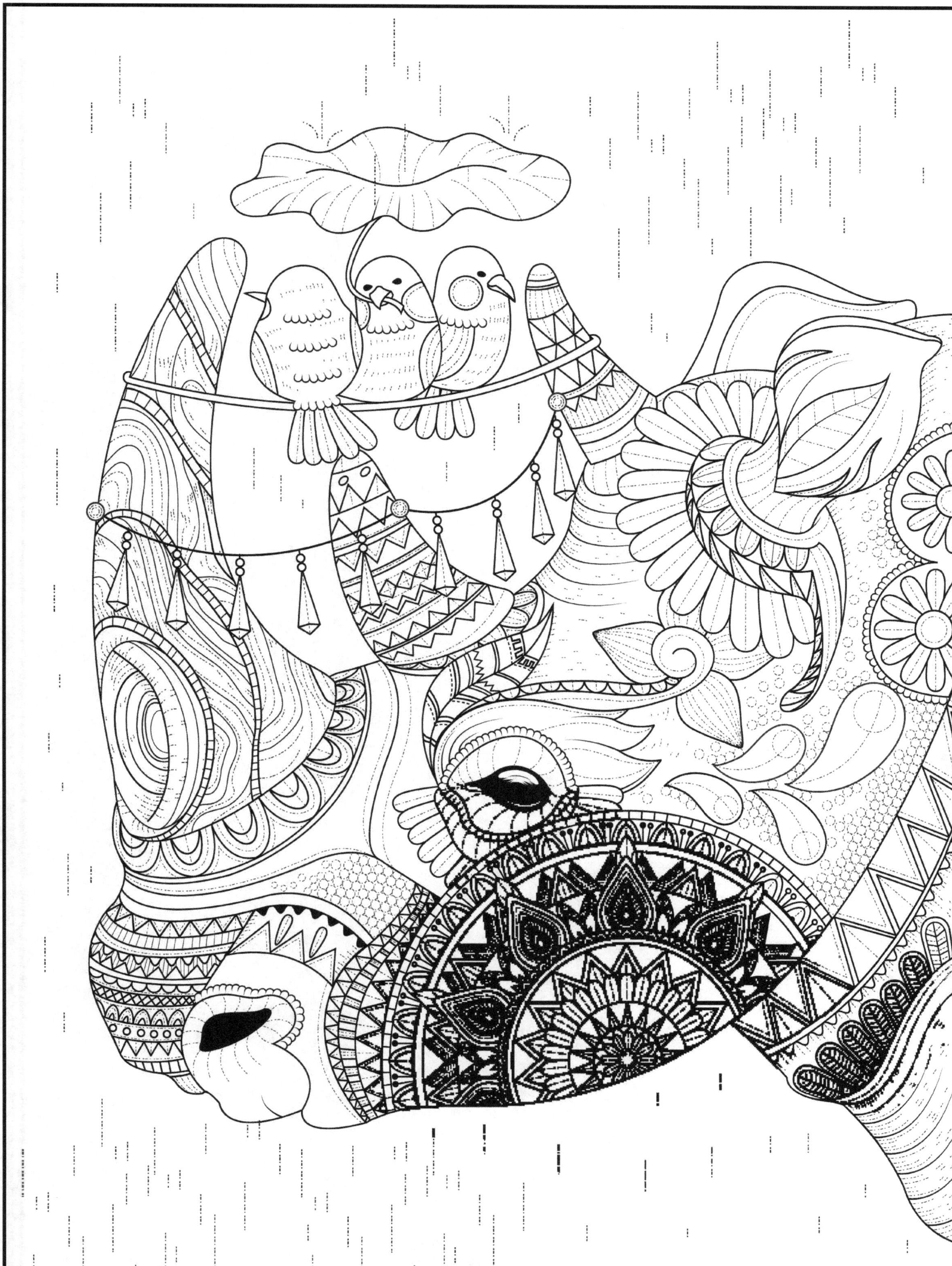

Thank you for purchasing this coloring book! I hope that you enjoy coloring it as much as I enjoyed creating it. Please consider leaving a review, I really appreciate hearing your opinion!

Sign-Up to Get a Free Coloring Book

Subscribe to our newsletter and get a free printable coloring book of some of our most popular illustrations. Plus you'll receive special offers, sneak peeks at new releases, and more. Visit us at **www.creativecoloring.co** for details.

We want to hear from you!

We hope you've enjoyed this coloring book and that is brings you many hours of fun, stress relief, and creativity. We'd love to see and share your creations.

Send us your ideas, suggestions, and finished artwork:

www.creativecoloring.co
facebook.com/creativecoloringpress
Instagram: @creativecoloringpress
Twitter: @creativecoloringpress

Bonus

Turn the page for bonus pages from some of our most popular coloring books.

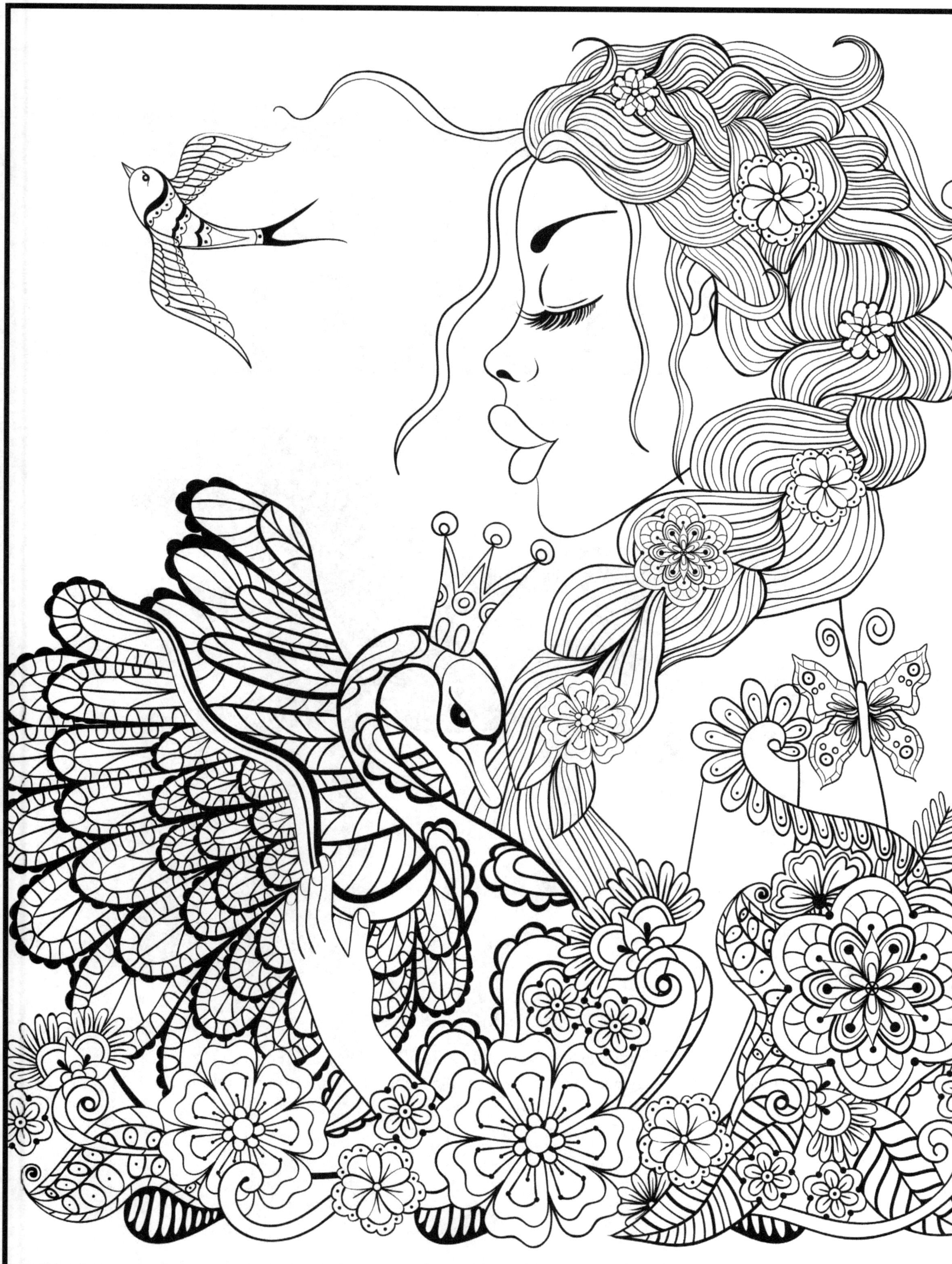

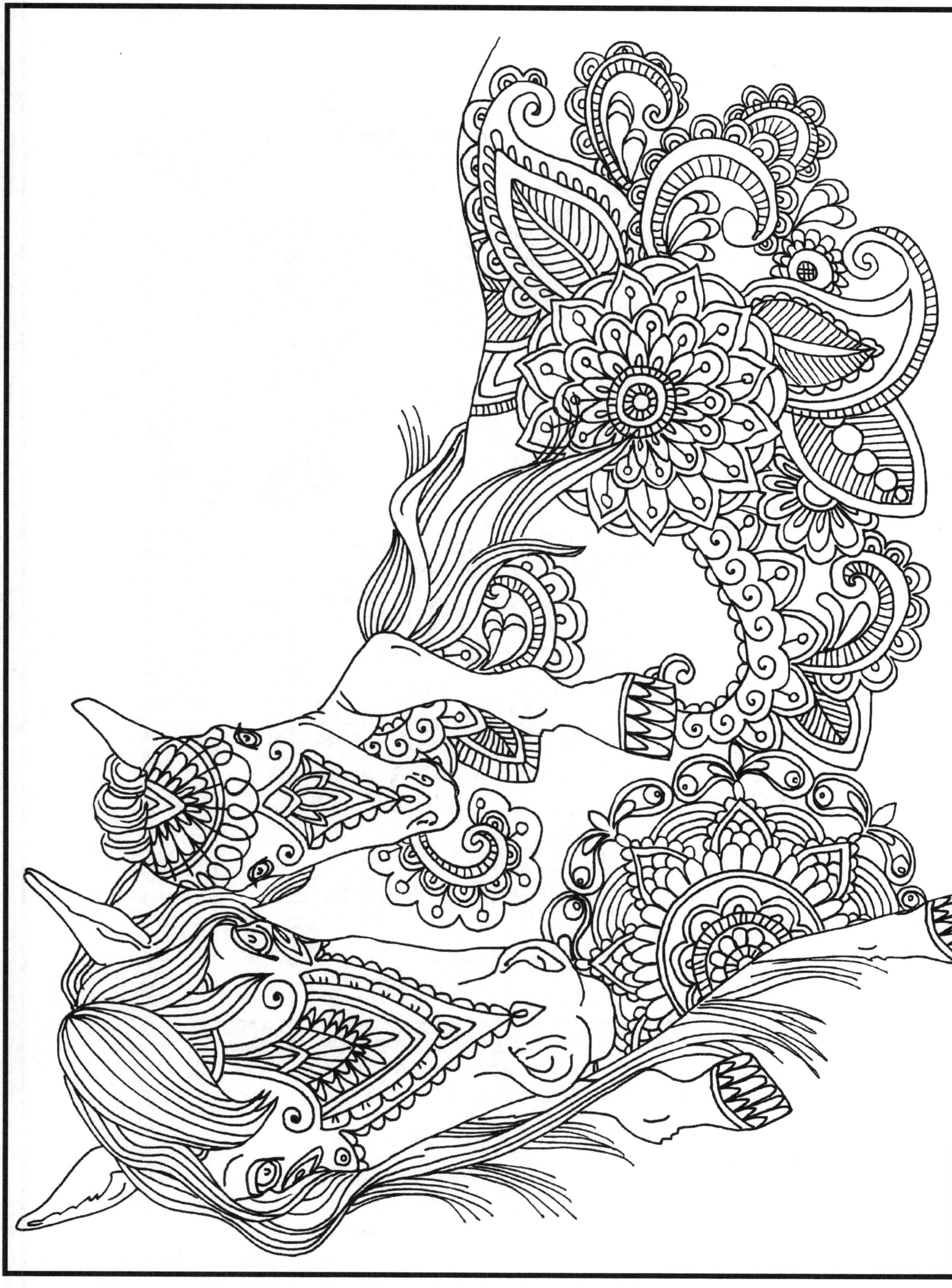

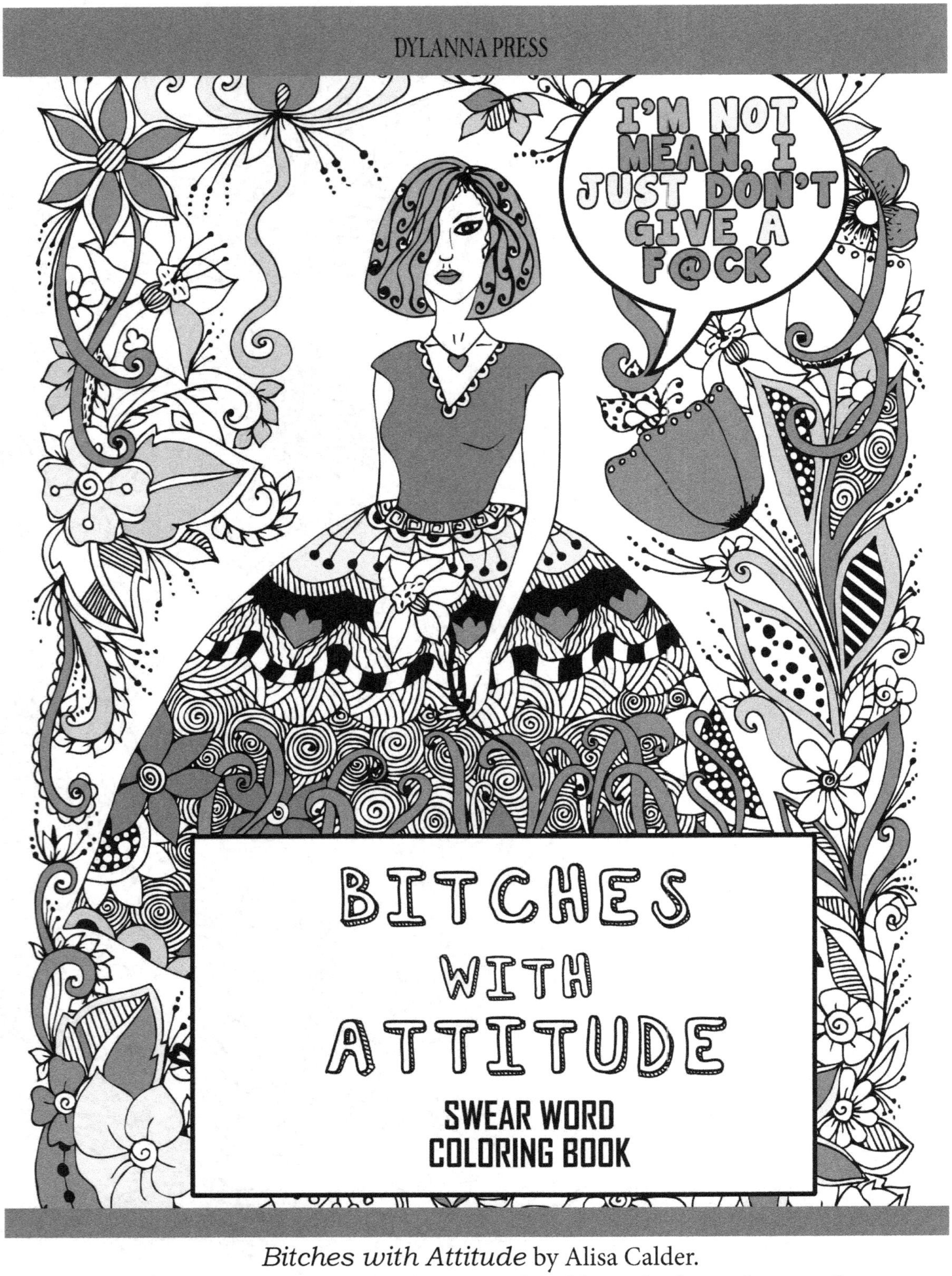
DYLANNA PRESS
I'M NOT MEAN, I JUST DON'T GIVE A F@CK
BITCHES WITH ATTITUDE
SWEAR WORD COLORING BOOK

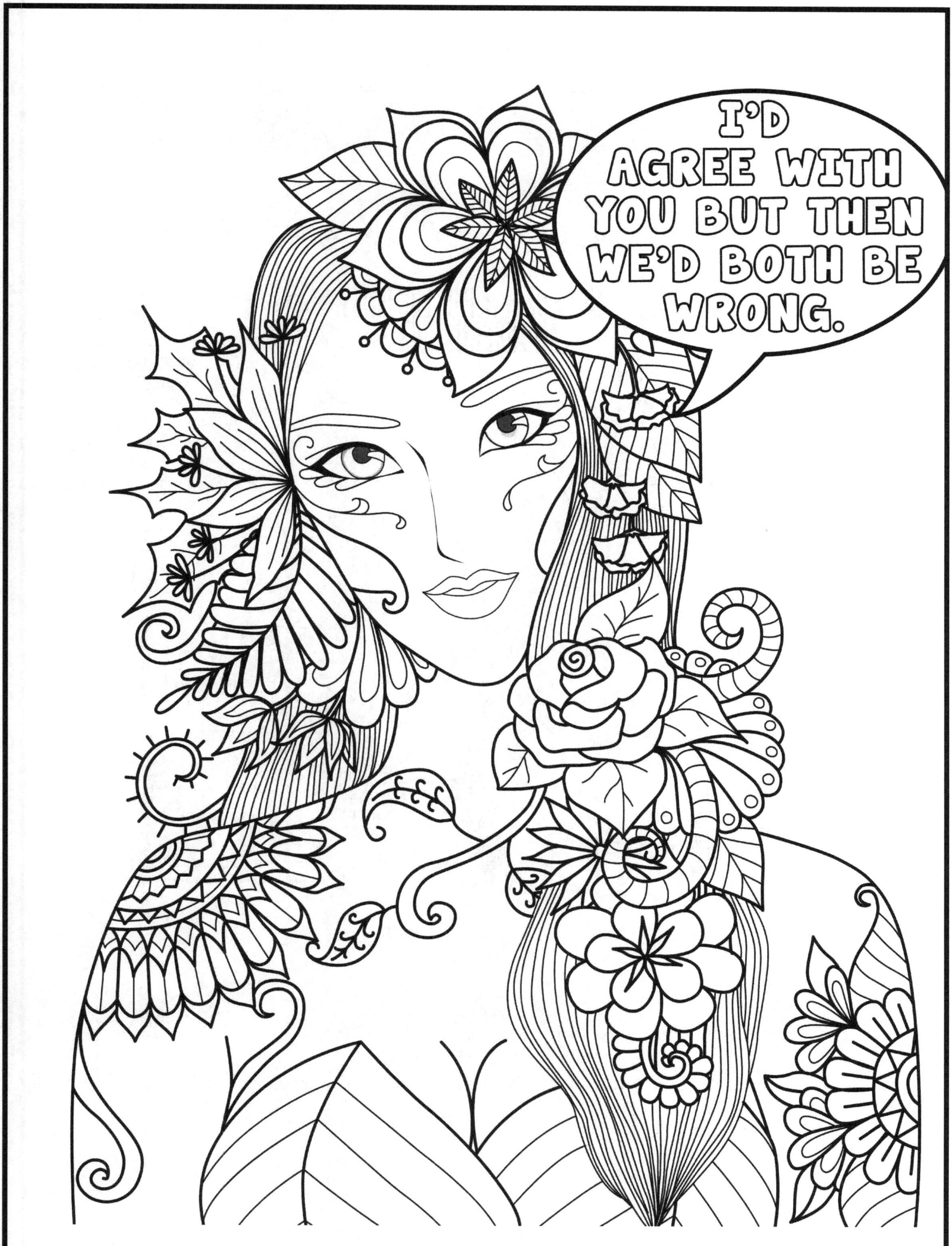
I'D AGREE WITH YOU BUT THEN WE'D BOTH BE WRONG.

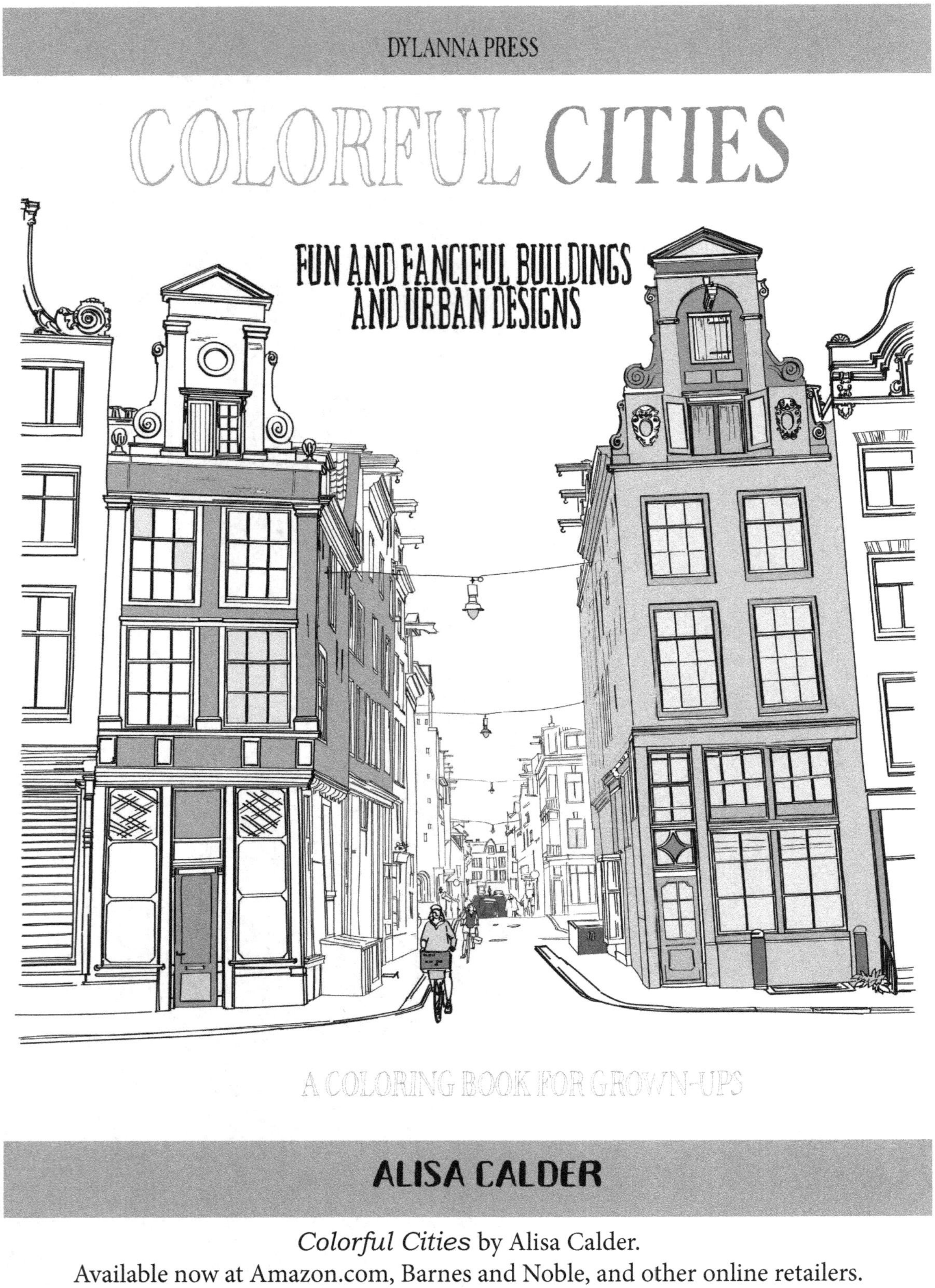
DYLANNA PRESS
COLORFUL CITIES
FUN AND FANCIFUL BUILDINGS AND URBAN DESIGNS
A COLORING BOOK FOR GROWN-UPS
ALISA CALDER

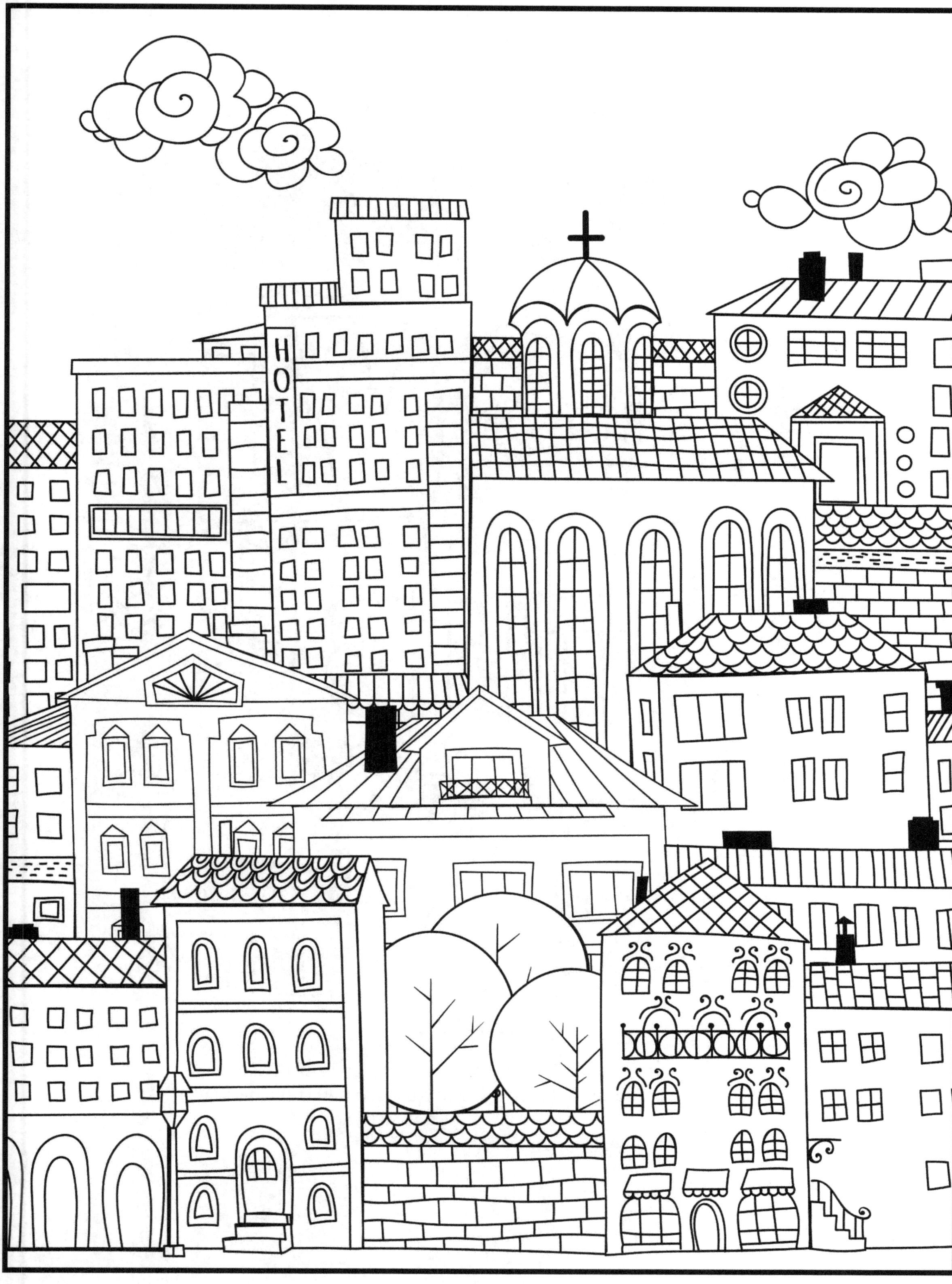
HOTEL

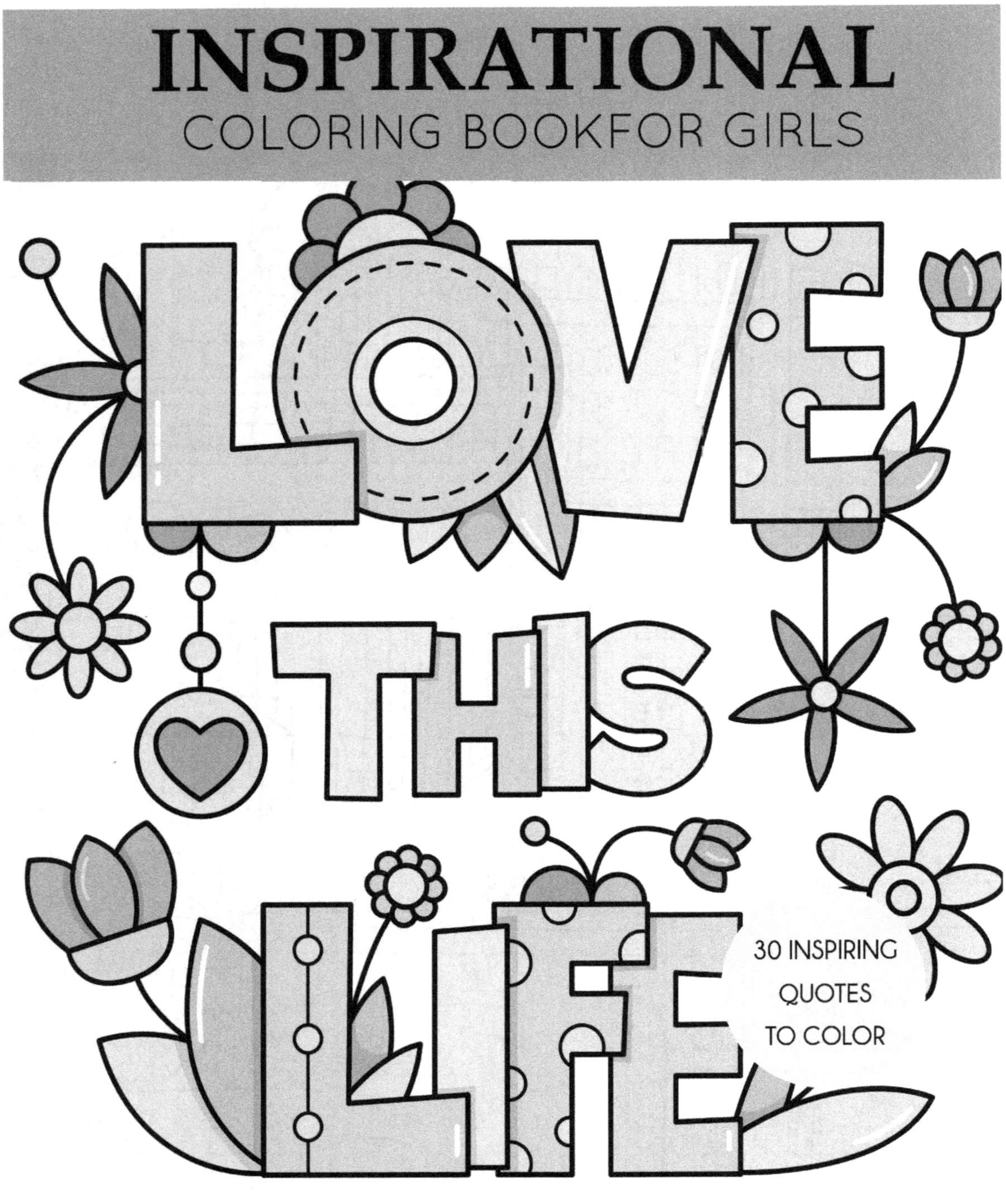

Inspirational Coloring Book for Girls by Alisa Calder.
Available now at Amazon.com, Barnes and Noble, and other online retailers.

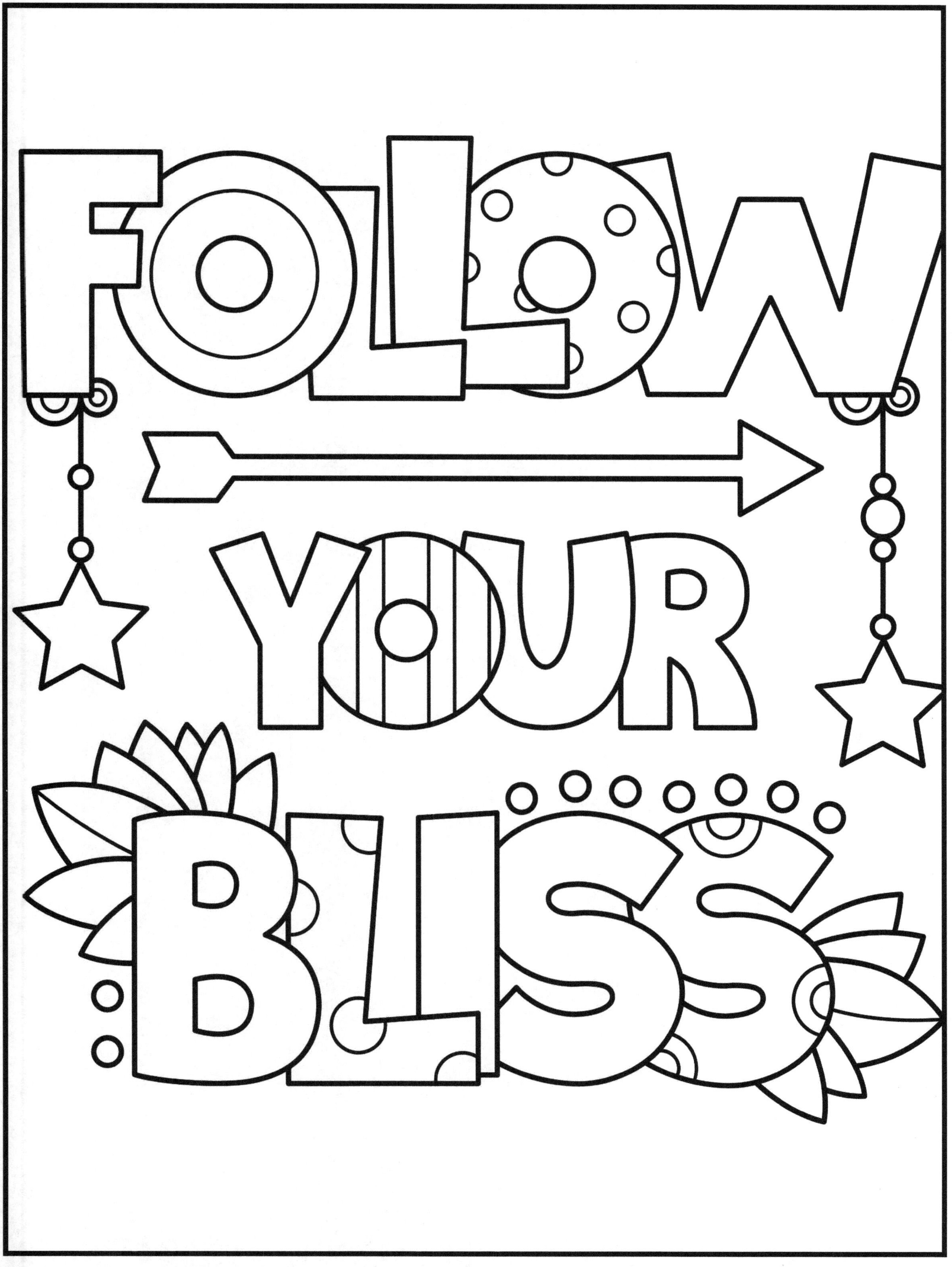
FOLLOW
YOUR
BLISS

CPSIA information can be obtained
at www.ICGtesting.com
Printed in the USA
LVHW061000250220
648138LV00016B/415

9 781942 268932